Kokopelli

Fluteplayer Images in Rock Art

Dennis Slifer & James Duffield

Ancient City Press
Santa Fe, New Mexico

Grateful acknowledgment is made to the following people for permission to reprint their works: Solala Towler for his poem, *Cocopeli Stories*; Sharman Apt Russell for *Songs of the Fluteplayer*; Ann Zwinger for *Wind in the Rock*; Linda Lay Shuler for *She Who Remembers*; Terry Tempest Williams for "Kokopelli's Return"; John Neary for "Kokopelli Kitsch"; and Clay Johnson for "Clay's Tablet (Barrier Canyon)."

Color Plate 5: Photo by David Grant Noble

International Standard Book Number
0-941270-80-7

Book design by Shadow Canyon Graphics

Cover Illustration by Elizabeth Kay

Cover design by Connie Durand

Library of Congress Cataloging-in-Publication Data

Slifer, Dennis.
　　Kokopelli: fluteplayer images in rock art / Dennis Slifer and James Duffield. — 1st ed.
　　　　p.　cm.
　　Includes bibliographical references and index.
　　ISBN 0-941270-80-7 (pbk.)
　　1. Pueblo Indians—Art. 2. Rock art—Southwest, New. 3. Pueblo Indians—Legends. 4. Pueblo Indians—Antiquities. 5. Southwest, New—Antiquities.
　　　. I. Title.
E99.P9S58　1993
709'.01'130979—dc20
　　　　　　　　　　　　　　　　　　　　　　93-43122
　　　　　　　　　　　　　　　　　　　　　　CIP

10　9　8　7　6

Contents

Preface   *v*

Acknowledgments   *viii*

Solala Towler, Cocopeli Stories   *ix*

INTRODUCTION   *1*

Sharman Apt Russell, Songs of the Fluteplayer   *15*

**THE MANY GUISES AND RELATIONS OF
THE HUMPBACKED FLUTEPLAYER**   *17*

Ann Zwinger, Wind in the Rock   *35*

FLUTEPLAYER IMAGES IN ROCK ART   *37*

Linda Lay Shuler, She Who Remembers   *107*

FLUTEPLAYER IMAGES IN CERAMICS AND KIVA MURALS   *109*

Terry Tempest Williams, "Kokopelli's Return"   *121*

MYTHS AND STORIES   *123*

John Neary, "Kokopelli Kitsch"   *137*

CONCLUSION   *139*

Clay Johnson, "Clay's Tablet (Barrier Canyon)"   *141*

Notes   *143*

References   *151*

Glossary   *161*

Appendix: Drawings   *169*

Index   *185*

The Authors   *199*

Preface

There was a time when, as geologists, we were satisfied to make occasional halts at roadside outcrops to investigate the rock and fossil possibilities, or even to walk several miles to have a closer look at an interesting geological formation. That time of relative innocence is now a thing of the past, since the rock art "obsession" has befallen us. These days we find it difficult, if not impossible, to bypass a promising-looking, well-patinated escarpment or boulder field without at least scanning the area with binoculars.

Happily, we have learned through our membership in the American Rock Art Research Association that we are not alone in being so obsessed. One of us attended a symposium of the Utah Rock Art Research Association in September of 1992; he was delighted to find himself in the midst of so many persons of kindred spirit. The convocation of the 1994 International Rock Art Congress in Flagstaff, Arizona, underlines the scope of worldwide interest in the subject.

We have spent many weeks over a period of several years roaming the mountain and desert Southwest—afoot, by four-wheel-drive vehicle, by raft and canoe, and occasionally by mountain bike—searching for the ultimate rock art creation. Our campsites were often remote. We found many amazing petroglyph and pictograph panels, left hundreds or even thousands of years ago by Indian artists. Often the meaning or purpose of rock art is obscure; nevertheless, many of these sites are still considered sacred by contemporary Native Americans. This mysterious quality, when combined with the artistic and ideological aspects of these creations, provides us with an endless source of inspiration and fascination.

After devoting much time and effort to these explorations, which often involved climbing steep ledges and talus slopes, dodging rattlesnakes and cactus, and coping with the usual heat, dust, insects, and thunderstorms common to the area, we decided to concentrate our attention on a fascinating character we found occurring with increasing frequency on rock art panels during our rambles. Further research into his nature has revealed to us why he was of such importance to prehistoric peoples. At Hopi, his name is Kokopelli.

We hope this book, describing Kokopelli in all his roles and aspects, will be of interest to archaeologists as well as the general public, especially at a time when rock art is becoming such a popular subject for investigation. In the past, archaeologists have often neglected to record rock art at sites under survey or excavation, this omission primarily due to the difficulty of dating such panels. Today, the recording of rock art has apparently become an integral part of site surveys and "digs," thanks to the development of new dating techniques, and also because of the growing realization that rock art, through its iconographic and ideological aspects, is a valuable key to explaining the social and cultural dynamics of prehistoric Indian societies.

Nearly all photographs in the book are the work of the authors; exceptions are properly credited. The drawings were made as accurately as possible, by tracing images in photographs or previously published illustrations. Panels of crowded elements have occasionally been edited for clarity.

Now, in imminent danger of exhausting available rock art sites to record in New Mexico and adjacent areas, the authors (one of whom recently participated in a rock art trip to Baja California) are looking forward with great anticipation to expanding their knowledge of such sites in other parts of the world.

ACKNOWLEDGMENTS

We owe our gratitude to friends and colleagues who have assisted in this project. Curt and Polly Schaafsma provided site information, photographs, and advice. Others who shared information about sites are David Grant Noble, Sally Cole, Ike Eastvold, Jesse Warner, Hugh and Margie Crouse, Charlie DeLorme, Jim Mullany, Eula Payne, Bill Davis, Jim and Luann Hook, John Young, Betty Lilienthal, Janet Leslie, Joseph Villegas, Ellen McGehee, Beverly Larson, Tony Lutonski, and Nancy Wier.

For company and assistance on some of our field trips, we thank Wyatt Harris, Eric Drew, Eric Renner, Nancy Spencer, Jeff Nelson, and Dena Slifer.

The library research at the New Mexico Laboratory of Anthropology would not have been possible without the expert assistance of Laura Holt and Tracey Kimball.

Jeff Nelson generously printed many of our black-and-white photographs, and also made available some of his own images. David G. Noble also granted permission to use some of his photographs, as did Janet Golio and Joseph Cramer.

Rolleen Stricker and Jay Maurer were helpful in reviewing and commenting on early drafts of the manuscript.

Finally, we extend our thanks to Mary Powell of Ancient City Press, who agreed to publish the work of two rock art enthusiasts.

Cocopeli played on and on,
and if he hadn't been so lost
in his song
he would have heard the sound
of water dripping off the branches
all around him,
or the steady thumping
as huge loads of snow
slid off the tired limbs.
Little by little
the snow receded,
revealing tiny patches
of new green grass,
which got bigger and bigger
as more of the snow melted. . . .
One by one
birds started joining in
on Cocopeli's song
until there was a whole chorus
cheeping right along.
The other animals started peeking out
from behind the bushes and trees.
They were all overjoyed

that Spring had finally come
to their part of the forest.
Very timid and frightened at first,
they came out into the clearing
where Cocopeli stood playing,
still unaware
of the effect of his music.
When Cocopeli stopped
he found himself surrounded
by happy thankfull animals
and all the snow and cold gone.
He looked around, astonished,
until he realized what had happened.

A great Elk,
who was one of the bravest
of the forest dwellers,
summoned up her courage
and stepped forward.
"We who dwell in this forest
thank you," she said,
"for chasing away the Long Winter."

—Solala Towler,
Cocopeli Stories

Introduction

Throughout the continent, but particularly in the desert Southwest, prehistoric Native Americans left a fascinating visual record through their rock art: images, many of them thousands of years old, carved or painted on stone surfaces. At hundreds of sites scattered throughout the mountains and deserts of the Southwest—on cliffs and boulders, and in caves—the ancient people recorded eloquently their visions and prayers.

Although rock art is found in places that were used for a variety of purposes, including habitation, food gathering, and hunting, most rock art has ritual or ceremonial origins, and many rock art sites are held to be sacred by present-day Native Americans. In many cases, however, rock art also appears to be a visual communication and documentation system that may mark trails, boundaries, and other features, as well as record time and events.

There are basically two kinds of rock art—petroglyphs and pictographs. Petroglyphs are pecked or carved images, whereas pictographs are painted onto rocks with natural pigments, usually in caves or under ledges. The symbols used in these ancient petroglyphs and pictographs represent a great diversity of meanings, traditions, beliefs, and activities. The glyphic figures attract us, and speak through the centuries about other cultures' physical and spiritual worlds. They speak of magic, power, and awe, from a place and time that we can often only imagine.

From the period of small bands of early hunter-gatherers to that of later, and more complex, agricultural societies, rock art continued to be produced in constantly evolving styles, until there came to exist a bewildering array of stylistic elements in rock art—abstract, geometric, and representational.

The "Golden Age" of southwestern rock art is long past; nevertheless, there are ethnographic records and stylistic/iconographic evidence of Native Americans maintaining this tradition in historic times. At Zuni, and perhaps sporadically elsewhere in the Southwest, rock art creation continues to this day. Although he is unlikely to be found in contemporary rock art, there is one unmistakable, wide-ranging figure who appears frequently on prehistoric panels— the mythic being or supernatural known popularly as Kokopelli.

The Humpbacked Fluteplayer

One of the most intriguing and widespread images found in southwestern rock art is the humpbacked fluteplayer, a mythic figure commonly known as Kokopelli. Easily identified amongst other images, there is something archetypal, whimsical, and universally appealing about this character. Although he appears in an amazing variety of forms, he typically possesses some characteristic traits that distinguish him. Kokopelli's flute, humped back, and prominent phallus are his trademarks. These features and the widely held beliefs that Kokopelli was a fertility symbol, roving minstrel or trader, rain priest, hunting magician, trickster, and seducer of maidens, have contributed to his popularity. Although much has been written about Kokopelli, an aura of mystery persists about this ancient character. He is one of the few prehistoric deities to have survived in recognizable form from Anasazi times to the present.[1]

Images of fluteplayers occur in prehistoric rock art, ceramics, and murals over a large area of the American Southwest (Fig. 1). That this symbol is prevalent throughout such a large area and for more than a thousand years suggests that the fluteplayer character was quite significant in prehistoric times. Many fluteplayer images in rock art occur within the territory of the Anasazi, or "Ancient Ones," of the Four Corners area on the Colorado Plateau. The Anasazi were primarily a horticultural society, growing corn, beans, and squash for their food staples. Spectacular cliff dwellings and multistoried masonry pueblos with underground ceremonial chambers called kivas are the architectural tradition of the classic Anasazi Period. The Anasazi tradition spans a period from at least as early as 200 B.C. to approximately A.D. 1540, when the Spanish entered the Southwest. Modern Pueblo peoples living along the

Rio Grande, at Hopi, Zuni, and at Acoma, are descendants of the Anasazi. The Hopi clans are apparently descended from the Sinagua as well as from the Anasazi (see page 83).

The Basketmaker Period of the Anasazi preceded the Pueblo Period, the latter commencing around A.D. 700 (Fig. 2). Both periods have included the humpbacked fluteplayer in their pantheon of deities or supernaturals. Fluteplayers are also seen in the iconography of the Hohokam of southern Arizona (ca. 300 B.C.. to A.D. 1450), the Mogollon of southern New Mexico (A.D. 100 to A.D. 1400), and the Fremont of eastern Utah (A.D. 400 to A.D. 1350; see Figure 2). The most numerous examples of fluteplayer images in rock art occur near the well-known Anasazi cultural centers of Chaco Canyon and Canyon de Chelly, and throughout the drainages of the Rio Grande, San Juan, and Colorado rivers and their tributaries.

Exactly when they first appear is uncertain, but nonphallic fluteplayers without humps are present in Basketmaker III rock art dating back to around A.D. 500.[2] After A.D. 1000 they are present with hump and flute in Anasazi rock art, pottery, and wall paintings. They also appear on ceramics of the Mimbres in southern New Mexico around A.D. 1000 to A.D. 1150 and on Hohokam pottery by A.D. 750 to A.D. 850.[3]

The fluteplayer's origin is lost in time, but some believe the tradition may have come north from ancient Mexico or South America with itinerant traders carrying their goods in sacks (humps?) on their backs.[4] These southern traders, known as *pochtecas*, were from an Aztec merchant guild and power base that operated at Casas Grandes (Chihuahua,

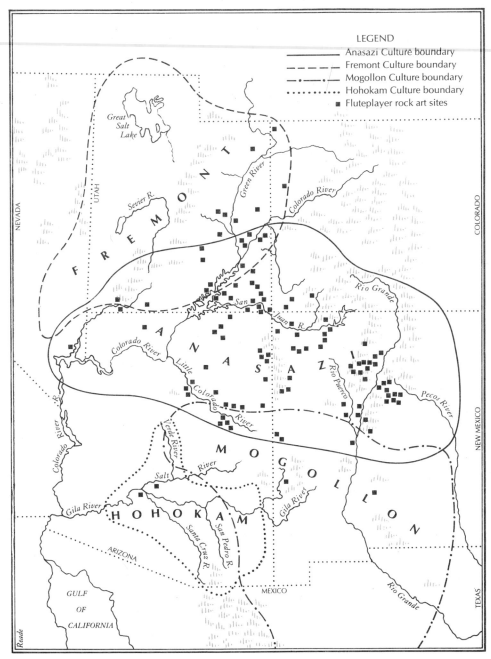

Figure 1
Map of prehistoric cultural divisions in the Four Corners region, showing locations of rock art sites with fluteplayer images. Adapted from Schaafsma, 1980. Used with permission.

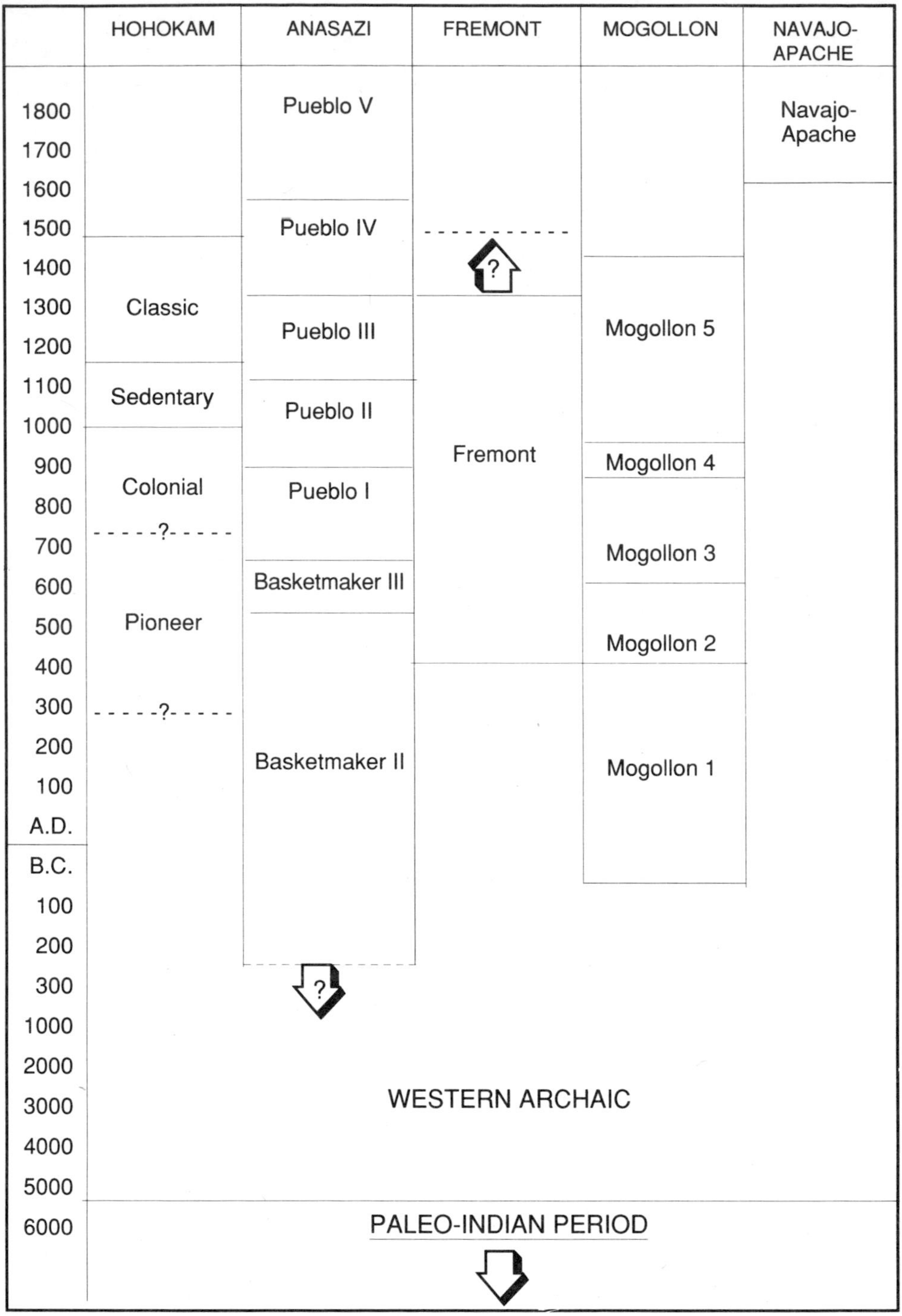

	HOHOKAM	ANASAZI	FREMONT	MOGOLLON	NAVAJO-APACHE
1800		Pueblo V			Navajo-Apache
1700					
1600					
1500		Pueblo IV	- - - - - - - - - -		
1400			?		
1300	Classic	Pueblo III		Mogollon 5	
1200					
1100	Sedentary	Pueblo II			
1000					
900			Fremont	Mogollon 4	
800	Colonial	Pueblo I			
700	- - - - -?- - - - -			Mogollon 3	
600		Basketmaker III			
500	Pioneer			Mogollon 2	
400					
300	- - - - -?- - - - -				
200		Basketmaker II		Mogollon 1	
100					
A.D.					
B.C.					
100					
200					
300		?			
1000					
2000					
3000		WESTERN ARCHAIC			
4000					
5000					
6000		PALEO-INDIAN PERIOD			

Figure 2
Chronology of southwestern prehistoric culture groups. Adapted from Schaafsma, 1980. Used with permission.
(Note: Basketmaker I is now considered to be an extension of Western Archaic culture.)

Mexico) and throughout the Chihuahuan Desert from about A.D. 1200 to A.D. 1400, and were at the nexus of relationships between the Southwest and ancient Mexico. In addition to packs, these traders carried walking sticks or canes, which they venerated. Canes and crooked sticks are portrayed in rock art of the Mogollon, Hohokam, and Anasazi, and also figure prominently in modern Pueblo ceremony as badges of office, prayer-stick bundles, and altar pieces. The long-distance trade networks of the *pochtecas* apparently helped spread cultural and religious elements between Mexico and the Southwest.

The *pochteca* era, insofar as southwestern rock art iconography is concerned, was perhaps mainly the inspiration for humpbacked (or burden-basket bearing) figures with crooks or canes rather than for fluteplayer images per se. The fluteplayer appeared in rock art of this region hundreds of years before the main influx of traders from the south. Apparently, the humpbacked fluteplayer, whether phallic or not, was essentially a phenomenon which developed in the Southwest, perhaps originating on the Colorado Plateau where such a profusion of fluteplayer depictions is found. The trader/*pochteca* hypothesis for Kokopelli's origin is further discussed in Section II.

In Pueblo myths, Kokopelli carries in his hump seeds, babies, and blankets to offer to maidens that he seduces. In the upper Rio Grande pueblos, he wandered between villages with a bag of songs on his back. As a fertility symbol, he was welcome during corn-planting season and was sought after by barren wives, although avoided by shy maidens. In the Andes of South America, medicine men still wander between villages with flutes and sacks of corn.[5]

The ancient Kokopelli prototype may have been responsible for carrying maize to the American Southwest and introducing it to the local cultures. Pod corn (tunicate maize), a primitive type of corn thought to possess healing properties, was essentially unknown in prehistoric North America, but some ears of it have been found near Betatakin ruins in Tsegi Canyon, Arizona.[6] An ethnobotanist has claimed that where pod corn has been found at prehistoric sites in the Southwest, there are often nearby petroglyphs of the humpbacked fluteplayer.[7]

The humpbacked fluteplayer has various names among modern Pueblos, but it is the Hopi name Kokopelli that is best known. Other variations of this name are Kokopilau, Kokopele, Kokopeltiyo, and Kokopelmana (the female version). Kokopelli, the Hopi *kachina* ("respected spirit"), is associated with fertility and rain; has a hump and a long snout (but no flute); and was originally phallic.[8] The name "Kokopelli" appears to be of combined Zuni/Hopi origin, probably translated literally as "kachina hump."

The kachina cult, a ceremonial complex that involves the impersonation of spiritual beings by masked dancers, was probably directly adopted (or acquired in an ideologically selective manner) by the Pueblo peoples from the Mogollon in the fourteenth century.[9] Kachinas are benevolent supernaturals who serve as intermediaries between the gods and man to bring rain, fertility, and good health. It is likely that the modern Kokopelli kachina has evolved from the prehistoric lineage of diverse fluteplayers portrayed in rock art and pottery throughout the Southwest.

Not all fluteplayers or humpbacks should be confused with the Hopi kachina, but common usage and

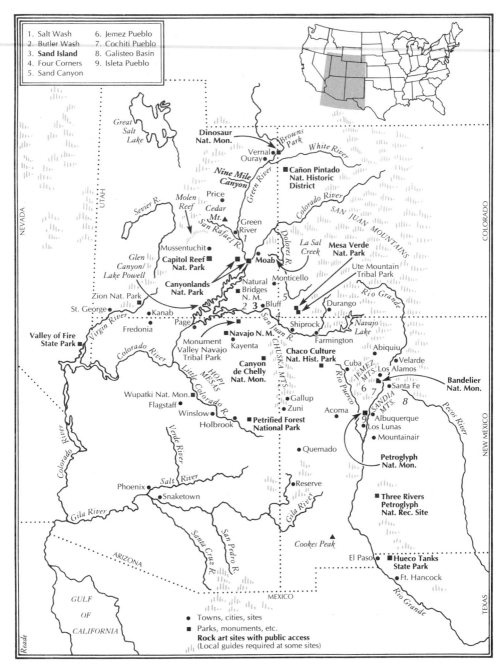

1. Salt Wash
2. Butler Wash
3. **Sand Island**
4. Four Corners
5. Sand Canyon
6. Jemez Pueblo
7. Cochiti Pueblo
8. Galisteo Basin
9. Isleta Pueblo

● Towns, cities, sites
■ Parks, monuments, etc.
Rock art sites with public access
(Local guides required at some sites)

Figure 3
Geographical map of the Southwest showing selected rock art sites with designated public access.

great contemporary popularity have indelibly affixed Kokopelli's name to these images. While the distinction may be important—and the Hopi kachina is later discussed in detail—the Kokopelli name is used in the popular sense herein to refer to prehistoric fluteplayer images.

In addition to the fluteplayer images described in this survey, there are more that have been recorded and perhaps hundreds of others waiting to be discovered.

In the Four Corners region of the Southwest, the primary focus of this book, most rock art sites are found within the drainages of the Colorado and Rio Grande rivers and their tributaries (the San Juan, Green, Little Colorado, and Dolores). These sites are frequently located at canyon mouths, on mesa tops, and around habitation sites, seasonal camps, and trails. Nearly all are found where there is at least an intermittent water supply. Most sites face in a southerly direction, where they are less affected by lichen growth and rock surface deterioration.

Visiting Rock Art Sites

Rock art is a valuable resource, from which much can be learned about the ancient artists and their cultures. However, the ancient petroglyphs and pictographs of the Southwest and of other areas in the United States are a fragile and endangered resource.

Some rock art may last for thousands of years if well protected from exposure to the elements that gradually deteriorate all rock art. Unfortunately, careless and in some cases malicious human activity is an even greater threat than wind, rain, lichen growth, and other weathering agents.

Rock art should never be touched, since the salt, moisture, and oils from our skin will hasten deterioration of both petroglyphs and pictographs. Chalk or other material should not be used to highlight rock art for photography, as they may hasten or retard the natural patination process of the rock; and application of chalk and other marking material obfuscates the relative dating of overlapping images. Further, the person applying the chalk may incorrectly interpret dim or faded portions of a design, thereby giving erroneous impressions to subsequent viewers. Likewise, making rubbings of petroglyphs is ultimately damaging because the rock is unnaturally eroded, and patination, lichen growth, and other natural processes are disrupted by repetitive stress and placement of adhesive tapes. The conservation adage, "Take nothing but pictures, leave nothing but footprints," is especially true for visiting rock art sites.

Bullet holes and graffiti are sad and fairly common conditions encountered at many rock art sites today. Increasingly, we also see evidence of stolen rock art, where fresh scars from chisels and broken-out slabs of rock mark the previous location of a petroglyph (Fig. 4). These shameful attempts to remove examples of our prehistoric heritage often result in destruction of the sought-after treasure, as the rock usually fractures into small pieces. Presumably, such criminal activity is motivated by a market for authentic rock art.

As rock art popularity increases, so does the number of people visiting sites. Sometimes the sheer number of visitors, although mostly well intentioned, has an adverse impact on sites. For instance, photographers have built bonfires in front of panels to obtain

Figure 4
Vandalized petroglyph
panel, Galisteo Basin,
New Mexico.

dramatic lighting effects; this harms the rock art
through smoke damage or thermally induced exfolia-
tion of the rock surface. Likewise, the burning of
votive candles and incense can damage sensitive sites,
especially those in caves. In the Los Padres National
Forest of California, Chumash Indian pictograph
sites have been recently closed to visitors for such rea-
sons. Soil erosion due to foot traffic around heavily
visited sites can also alter original conditions and
damage archaeologically significant features.

Much rock art is on public land in the West and is
protected by federal and state antiquity laws; but
enforcement at many remote sites is difficult. Because
of this problem, information about the precise location of rock art sites is rarely given in publications in
order to protect the resource. The authors continue
this tradition here by providing only general, never
specific, locations of rock art sites.

Those who wish to visit some of the sites mentioned in this book should inquire at the appropriate land management agencies (National Park Service, U.S. Bureau of Land Management, U.S. Forest Service, state parks, etc.) where the rock art sites occur. Always obtain permission from owners of private property before visiting sites on their land.

If you visit a rock art site, do so with the utmost care and respect. Do not trespass without the landowner's permission. Tread lightly and do not touch the rock art—ever. Behave as if you were in a sacred place. Be open to your senses, pay attention to your surroundings, and listen for the faint voices of the ancients.

. . . I was alone and the fluteplayer came upon me suddenly, unsought and unplanned. Surrounded only by rock and sky and desert, the glimpse of a petroglyph can be like the sighting of a wild and possibly dangerous animal. It can stop your breath . . . in the canyon behind me wind whistled through scrub oak and smoothed the fractured surface of pink stone . . . this particular fluteplayer could well be a thousand years old, an age that hovered outside my range of belief. Here, drawn on a flat rock twenty miles from my home, the fluteplayer was caught in one of his many transformations into a bug or odd-shaped creature. Already his hump had formed the curved shell of a locust and his antenna streamed behind him as his arms shortened into an insect's legs . . . he had the power to repel and slightly frighten. . . .

Since then I have seen other Kokopellis, many of them, tootling under a high ledge at Canyon de Chelly or dancing among the ruins of Chaco Canyon.

— Sharman Apt Russell,
Songs of the Fluteplayer

The Many Guises and Relations of the Humpbacked Fluteplayer

There are probably thousands of Kokopelli images found at hundreds of rock art sites throughout the Southwest, and no two of them are exactly alike. This incredible variety is due in part to cultural differences through time and space, but also to the creativity and individuality of the ancient artists. The images range from crude stick figures to sophisticated and elaborately rendered designs of individuals in infinite guises and poses. Kokopelli occurs as a lone figure, in association with animals, in pairs, and in groups. He is shown standing, sitting, recumbent, kneeling, dancing to his flute music, being carried, and even making love (Fig. 5). He is sometimes shown hunting deer or

Figure 5
Petroglyph panel
showing Kokopelli in
fertility context,
La Cieneguilla,
New Mexico.

bighorn sheep, and in association with snakes, lizards, birds, and other animals. Nearly four hundred depictions of the character, from over eighty sites, have been documented in this survey.

These images share a number of interrelated attributes. Kokopelli has been interpreted by various authors as a deity, clan symbol, shaman or medicine man, trader, insect- or animal-like being, and as an individual with a spinal deformity. He is usually portrayed with a hump on his back, is often phallic in the extreme, and holds a flute to his mouth, sometimes appearing to dance to his tune. He often has feathers or antenna-like appendages on his head (Fig. 6), and may appear as a flute-playing insect or animal (Fig. 7).

Figure 6
Petroglyph,
La Cieneguilla,
New Mexico.
Photo by Jeff Nelson.

Figure 7
Petroglyph panel:
reclining fluteplayers
with insectlike
characteristics, Marsh
Pass area, Arizona.
From Kidder and
Guernsey, 1919.

Kokopelli and His Flute

There are rock art depictions of fluteplayers without the hump or phallus (Fig. 8), and there are hump-backed, phallic figures with no flute (Fig. 9). They may all be variations on the same theme, but the flute seems to be the most common diagnostic element.

Figure 8
Pictograph: reclining
fluteplayer, Navajo
National Monument,
Arizona.
After Schaafsma, 1966.

The flute is used in sacred ritual as well as for courtship in many cultures, and evidently had a special role in Anasazi culture; flutes made of bone and wood have been found among their artifacts.[1] Worked bird bone, possibly indicative of flutemaking, appeared as early as 200 B.C. in the Anasazi region. In prehistoric rock art of the Southwest, the

Figure 9
Petroglyph,
La Cieneguilla,
New Mexico.

flutes depicted are of the end-blown, direct type rather than the transverse, horizontally held variety. In addition to bone and wood flutes, others were fashioned from hollow reeds, especially in the Mogollon area. Coronado's expedition into the Pueblo area in 1540 found widespread use of flutes in celebrations; to accompany singing; and, by men, to entertain women while they worked.[2] It is also believed flutes were used as signaling devices and a means of communication. Traveling merchants in Mesoamerica used flutes and whistles to herald their presence.[3]

The Roles of Kokopelli

Kokopelli has been interpreted as a rain priest who calls the clouds with his flute, which he also plays to melt the snow and warm up the earth when appealed to by the sun-loving snakes.[4] He is often depicted

Figure 10
Petroglyph panel:
fluteplayer with snake,
north of Española,
New Mexico.

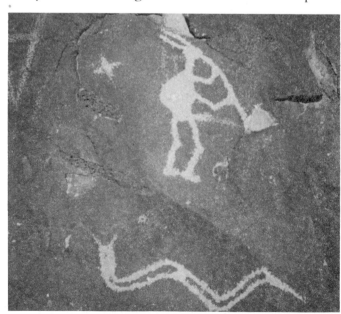

with snakes in rock art scenes (Fig. 10). The flute societies at Hopi play the flute over springs to bring rain.[5] Gourds for carrying water are sometimes attached to the ends of the Hopi flutes; some rock art depictions show a bulbous shape at the end of the flute (Fig. 11).[6] Kokopelli is portrayed along with

Figure 11
Petroglyph,
La Cieneguilla,
New Mexico.

moisture-loving creatures such as lizards or insects in rock art near Zuni, New Mexico (Fig. 12). The Zuni claim this association aids the magic in attracting moisture to that locale.[7] He has been associated with the locust, a patron of the Hopi Flute Society, and with the gray desert-robber fly, which is notorious for its enthusiastic copulation.[8]

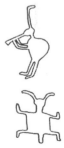

Figure 12
Petroglyph panel,
Zuni Reservation,
New Mexico.
After Young, 1988.

Figure 13
Pictograph panel
depicting phallic
hunters, Fire Temple
(kiva), Mesa Verde
National Park,
Colorado.
After Schaafsma,
1980.

A number of images of flute-playing animals are known. The horned mountain sheep depicted on a kiva mural at Fire Temple on Mesa Verde, Colorado (Fig. 13), have been linked to the hunting-priest aspect of the fluteplayer.[9] Kokopelli's fertility role extended to the animal world and ensured fecundity of the hunted game animals in particular. At the La Cieneguilla site near Santa Fe, New Mexico, there are numerous petroglyphs depicting Kokopelli as a hunter or warrior with bow and arrow (Fig. 14). One scene in the lower Santa Fe River Canyon (Fig. 15) contains a group of about twenty fluteplayers (cere-

Figure 14
Petroglyph panel
showing Kokopelli in
hunting context,
La Cieneguilla,
New Mexico.

Figure 15
Petroglyph panel
depicting numerous
archers and
fluteplayers,
lower Santa Fe River
Canyon, New Mexico.

mony, dance, hunting scene?), of which a dozen carry bows rather than flutes. Rock art images from elsewhere appear to depict the fluteplayer in the shape of indeterminate creatures (Figs. 16, 17, 18, A-1), perhaps suggesting shamanistic activities whereby various animal- or spirit-helper shapes are assumed by the fluteplayer as shaman.

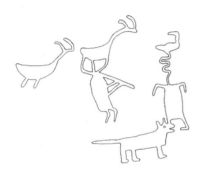

Figure 16 (left)
Petroglyphs: flyteplayers with zoomorphic attributes, Canyon de Chelly, Arizona. After Grant, 1978.

Figure 17 (right)
Petroglyph panel: zoomorphic fluteplayer, north of Española, New Mexico.

Figure 18
Petroglyph: zoomorphic fluteplayer, north of Española, New Mexico.

Whatever label we may attach to him—deity, priest, shaman, medicine man, healer, or magician—the fluteplayer's function was undoubtedly interrelated with creatures of the natural and supernatural worlds. The complexity and connectedness of all things in aboriginal mythology and spirituality preclude our ability to define and comprehend the exact meaning of the fluteplayer-animal relationships. Perhaps some things are better appreciated as mysteries.

The Origins and Migrations of Kokopelli

Anthropologist Jesse Walter Fewkes stated that migration accounts of the Hopi/Tewa indicate that the Kokopelli kachina was introduced by the Asa Clan, which wandered from the upper Rio Grande to Zuni, finally settling in Hopi at the end of the seventeenth century.[10] More recent rock art research suggests that the fluteplayer appeared at Hopi much earlier than this. The Asa Clan also lived for a time, during drought years, in Canyon de Chelly, where there are numerous rock art images of Kokopelli, many of which were possibly Asa Clan introductions (Fig. 19).[11]

Figure 19
Petroglyphs: fluteplayers
in fertility context,
Canyon de Chelly,
Arizona.
After Grant, 1978.

According to a Hopi informant,[12] Kokopelli is the totemic figure, or wuya, of the Asa Clan:

Kokopelli was a leader in old times who brought the people of Asa Clan from their home to Zuni, where they stopped. Those people who live [in Hopi] have their homes facing Zuni.

Campbell Grant has asserted that Kokopelli represents the Flute Clan.[13] A Hopi source identified the humpbacked fluteplayer in a Glen Canyon petroglyph as a Flute Clan symbol:

> Fluteplayer is clan symbol. Hunchback is a main leader in early times. Kokopelli was a regular man who did lots of good things and when he died was made into a kachina.[14]

This informant further identified the humpbacked fluteplayer as representing the Spider Clan, Water Clan, and Titmouse Clan:

> This clan, with this religion, went north and is supposed to warm up earth. Even flute playing all the time didn't help, and those people had to turn back, and when they get to Oraibi they put this religion up. Those people had lots of songs to make country warm. These clans Patkimyam [Water Clan] and Kokongyam [Tit-mouse (sic) Clan] have flutes . . . The Spider Clan came from north also.

In addition to being seen as a clan symbol, the humpbacked fluteplayer has also been described as an itinerant, flute-playing trader with a pack of goods on his back. Ek Chuah, a prehistoric Mayan deity, may have been "ancestral" to Kokopelli. He wears a backpack, carries a staff, and is patron of hunters, traveling merchants, and beekeepers.[15] Further, a trade network between the Aztecs of Mesoamerica and the ancient Pueblo peoples of the Southwest has been documented.[16]

Many Mesoamerican religious ideas probably reached the Southwest via these trade contacts. It is believed that early Mesoamerican traders of the trocador, or pochteca, type roamed as far north as the San Juan Basin—Chaco Canyon in particular—in the eleventh and twelfth centuries.[17] These traders exchanged parrots and macaws, among other things, for turquoise. Perhaps some of the backpacks depicted in rock art are meant to portray cages for the traders' birds. Kokopelli is shown along with bird images at a number of sites, but most often at La Cieneguilla, New Mexico. He is shown with a macaw perched on a hoop in a petroglyph at Fivemile Draw, Arizona (Color Plate 1). Macaws can also be identified in petroglyphs at Albuquerque's West Mesa site, Galisteo Basin sites, Chaco Canyon, and north of Española, New Mexico.

Kokopelli's Hump

Figure 20
Burden basket carriers
on Hohokam ceramics,
southern Arizona.
After Di Peso, 1974.

The hump can also be interpreted as a burden basket, which was employed throughout northern Mexico, and at Hopi was used along with a supporting forehead strap. Burden basket carriers are common in Hohokam ceramic motifs (Fig. 20). The burden basket was typically used by women for mundane purposes, but it is also associated with many kachinas and mythic beings. The hump on the fluteplayer's back, in addition to possibly being a trader's pack or a burden basket, could also represent a quiver for arrows, a ceremonial tablet or bustle, or another person or animal (Figs. 21-A and 21-B). A hunched or bent-over posture could also appear as humpbacked (Fig. 22). At the Tewa village of Hano at Hopi, Kokopelli's hump was thought to be filled with buck-

skin for shirts and moccasins to barter for brides. The Navajo deity Ghanaskidi has a humped back made of a rainbow, containing mist and seeds of all types of plants (A-71, also see Figure 27 [page 31]).[18]

Some images show a pendant or piggyback figure on the back of the fluteplayer, giving the illusion of a hump and raising the possibility that other hump-backed fluteplayers may have been drawn with stylized humps representing piggyback riders. In historical myths, humans, animals, and impersonations of animals carried on the back are common. At Acoma Pueblo, and among the eastern Apaches, there is a story of two brothers, one blind and one crippled. The blind brother carries the crippled one on his back in a cooperative effort to hunt.[19] The Zuni Eagle-Man brings rain and carries a sick boy on his back.[20] Slain game animals are carried on the backs of various kachinas at Hopi, Acoma, and Zuni.[21] Pendant figures are known from prehistoric rock art

Figure 22
Petroglyph: fluteplayer
in bent position, near
Quemado, New Mexico.
After Schaafsma, 1975.

Figure 23
Petroglyph: fluteplayer
with small figure on
hump, La Cieneguilla,
New Mexico.

as well as from ceramics. An interesting petroglyph at the La Cieneguilla, New Mexico, site shows a small figure attached to an existing hump on a fluteplayer's back (Fig. 23), giving the impression of a small spirit hovering nearby.

The back-shield, or tablet, worn in various Pueblo ceremonies may also be depicted as a hump in some prehistoric images. For example, Lenang, the Hopi Flute Kachina who sometimes lends his flute to Kokopelli, wears a moisture tablet (a painted skin stretched over a wooden framework and used for ritually making rain) on his back.[22] If such features were depicted in rock art, it would explain some of the oddly shaped and peculiarly placed humps on some figures in the Four Corners area. The hump-backed personage is widely associated with supernatural qualities in native myth and religion.[23] The Mesoamerican god-kings Quetzalcoatl, Moctezuma, and Xochiquetzal included humpbacks in their courts and entourages, where they provided religious consultation as well as entertainment. They were also in great demand as favored sacrificial subjects.[24] Humpbacks appear in the architecture, sculpture, and ceramics of ancient Mesoamerica as persons of apparent important social status.

Contemporary Kokopelli kachina dolls have a humpback rather than a pack or bag. This is the only historic kachina character with a humpback as an apparent physical deformity rather than a pack or bag worn on the back.[25]

Researchers G. B. Webb, Klaus F. Wellmann, and Joyce Alpert contend that the fluteplayer's hump is indicative of an individual suffering a spinal deformity such as that caused by Pott's disease.[26] A type of tuberculosis, Pott's disease produces kyphosis, an exaggerated convexity of the spine. The existence of tuberculosis in prehistoric America has been demonstrated by various scientists at a number of sites. Rock art scholars with medical backgrounds have examined paleopathological evidence along with the fluteplayer's traits to suggest this theory of Kokopelli's origin. In some rock art portrayals, he also seems to possess a clubfoot and misshapen or paralyzed legs, and is shown lying on his back playing the flute (Fig. 24). His erect phallus is further

Figure 24
Petroglyph panel:
recumbent fluteplayers,
Marsh Pass, Arizona.
From Kidder and
Guernsey, 1919.

explained as priapism, another symptom of Pott's disease whereby spinal cord disturbance results in permanent engorgement of the penis. Priapism would create the appearance of sexual prowess and supports the connection with Kokopelli's legendary fertility role. When embodied with the supernatural qualities of the humpback and the obvious fertility aspect, it is plausible that such individuals would be seen as special or powerful.

Kokopelli's Relatives

Kokopelli has several related characters among the iconography of groups such as the Hohokam, Navajo, and Mogollon.

The Hohokam were horticulturists who lived in villages in southern Arizona between about A.D. 300 and A.D. 1450 (see Figs. 1 and 2). They are known for their fine work in shell, bone, and stone, and also for their extensive use of irrigation.

Common among the design motifs of Hohokam ceramics are fluteplayers (Fig. 25) and figures carrying burden baskets on their backs. The Hohokam fluteplayer is usually shown alone, nonphallic, and with an arched back (but not with an unmistakable humpback).[27] He usually wears a headdress, presumably of feathers, which along with the flute suggests a nonsecular role. The Hohokam were painting fluteplayers on their pottery perhaps as early as the sixth century A.D., based on sherds from Snaketown, Arizona,[28] although there is now apparently a consensus placing the beginning of Hohokam culture sometime before A.D. 300 (with the earliest appearance of the fluteplayer in ceramics around A.D. 750 to A.D. 850). One of the Hohokam fluteplayers depicted on sherds from Snaketown appears to resemble an insectlike form (Fig. 26), which may suggest a connection between the Anasazi and Hohokam fluteplayers. The exact relationship between Hohokam fluteplayers and those of the Anasazi is unclear, but some postulate that the theme diffused from Mexican antecedents to the Hohokam and thence to the Anasazi by the Pueblo I Period—about A.D. 700.[29] Polly Schaafsma has recently proposed

Figure 25
Fluteplayer motif on Hohokam bowl, Snaketown, Arizona. After Bruggmann, 1989.

Figure 26
Ceramic design, partially reconstructed from sherds, Snaketown, Arizona. After Haury, 1976.

that the fluteplayer appeared in Anasazi rock art by around A.D. 500.[30] This theme appears to have been lost among the Hohokam by A.D. 1200.

The Navajo were Athabaskan-speaking nomadic peoples who entered the Southwest around A.D. 1500. As they spread through, and settled in, the Anasazi territory, they borrowed and modified some of the Puebloan ideology.

Ghanaskidi (Ghaan'ask'idii, or Ya ackidi) is a humpbacked Navajo supernatural, or ye'i, who represents a god of harvest, plenty, and mist.[31] He wears horns, carries a staff, and often has a humpback from which feathers radiate (Fig. 27). The hump is said to be made of the rainbow and contains mist or clouds and seeds of all kinds. He is equated with the mountain sheep, a valued game animal, and has similarities with Pang, the Hopi mountain sheep kachina. Both

Figure 27
Petroglyph panel:
Navajo Hump Back
God (Ghanaskidi),
Largo Canyon
drainage,
New Mexico.

Figure 28
Petroglyph:
zoomorphic fluteplayer,
Sand Island, Utah.
After Castleton, 1987.

Figure 29
Petroglyph:
humpbacked, phallic
figure with planting
cane (?),
Butler Wash, Utah.

Figure 30
Ceramics, Hohokam
"cane dancers,"
Arizona.
After Di Peso, 1974.

Pang and Ghanaskidi may be derived from the prehistoric humpbacked fluteplayer;[32] the former both wear headdresses of mountain sheep horns, have humps, and carry staffs. At Sand Island, near the town of Bluff, Utah, is a petroglyph of a flute-playing mountain sheep (Fig. 28). In the Navajo Night Chant myth, the hero's fingers freeze on his bow while waiting in ambush for mountain sheep, and he cannot shoot. The animals reveal themselves to be humpbacked gods and impart holy teachings to the hero. These gods are in charge of mountain sheep and make them available to the people.[33] Ghanaskidi is one of the most frequently depicted ye'is in the Navajo rock art of the Largo Canyon area near Four Corners. This rock art belongs to the Gobernador Phase, A.D. 1700 to A.D. 1775. Ghanaskidi is also depicted in Navajo sandpaintings.

Within the Mogollon culture region (consisting of two branches, the Jornada and Mimbres) depictions of humpbacked, and sometimes phallic, figures are found in rock art and ceramics, but none is playing the flute (see Fig. 189). They are included here because they seem very likely to be related to the humpbacked fluteplayer. Such figures can also be found within the territory of the Anasazi (Fig. 29), Hohokam (Fig. 30), and Apache (Fig. 31).

An interesting feature of some of these depictions is the crooked stick or staff, which is held. While some staffs probably represent ceremonial objects or badges of office similar to the scepter (Figs. 32 and A-3), the crook is thought to have fertility connotations and may actually represent a planting stick. Among the Anasazi rock art panels of southeastern Utah, some portray crooks in association with copulating couples,[34] and one petroglyph shows a figure holding both a flute and a crook (Fig. 33). There seems to be an obvious fertility aspect to the Mimbres Mogollon figure who is holding both crook and erect phallus with apparent glee (see Fig. A-4 and Section IV). In addition to the Anasazi and Mimbres examples, there are Hohokam ceramics showing figures carrying crooks and burden baskets (see Fig. 20).

The various aspects and multiple interpretations of Kokopelli and prehistoric images of humpbacked fluteplayers illustrate the complexity of the character. His origin and significance may never be fully understood, but enough is known to demonstrate his importance to the "Ancient Ones" and to ensure his contemporary popularity.

The great number and variety of prehistoric figures identified as Kokopelli are probably related through a continuum of mythic beings that has evolved and diffused throughout the Southwest over time. Whether such figures are identified as humpbacked fluteplayer, insect, mountain sheep, rainmaker, hunter, shaman, deity, hero, or fertility or clan symbol, it is understood that this prominent character is archetypal in the prehistoric art of the Southwest. The many different, yet possibly interchangeable, aspects of this character, both historic and prehistoric, illustrate the richness of the supernatural world of the indigenous people of the Southwest. Kokopelli is a fascinating fragment of that world, and, with his bag of gifts, flute, crook, numerous guises, animal friends, and libidinous activities, will continue to capture our imagination.

Figure 31
Pictograph:
humpbacked, phallic
figure with female
(Apache),
Hueco Tanks, Texas.

Figure 32
Petroglyph:
humpbacked figure
holding staff or cane,
La Cieneguilla,
New Mexico..

Figure 33
Petroglyph: phallic
fluteplayer with cane,
southeastern Utah.
After Manning, 1990.

... pecked into a dark varnished panel, are human figures, facing each other, dancing to the flute playing of Kokopelli, the priapic humpbacked fluteplayer. Except in this instance ... he has no hump, but the flute playing is unmistakable and the dancing figures are lively. Kokopelli is a familiar figure in Anasazi art and a striking one. ...

... Kokopelli appears as a combination Pied Piper and St. Francis of the canyons; he stands facing a mountain sheep that looks at him intently— mountain sheep are notoriously curious and I can well imagine one enticed to the sound of Kokopelli's flute. Perhaps Kokopelli enchants him, rendering him easier to kill. On another panel, far down the canyon, a butterfly-like shape takes flight near two atlatls while Kokopelli plays: a charm so that the atlatls would fly ... "like a butterfly," their aim true, the hunting good?

. . . Panels with Kokopelli have an enchanting animation, a vivacity, that the hieratic figures lack. I can almost hear the music of his flute, a trifle reedy in sound, but chuckling and full of delightful phrasing, irreverent and rollickingly suggestive.

—Ann Zwinger,
Wind in the Rock

Fluteplayer Images in Rock Art

Fluteplayer depictions in southwestern Indian rock art appear to have commenced as early as Basketmaker III times,[1] about A.D. 500 (Fig. 2), occurring with increasing frequency through the intervening centuries into the Pueblo V Period, the inception of which is marked by the entry of the Spanish into the Southwest about the middle of the sixteenth century. The Spanish colonial government and the Church did not actively suppress the Pueblo religion until early in the seventeenth century, around the time of the founding of Santa Fe on the site of an abandoned pueblo. So, in the Pueblo region at least, rock art traditions continued well into the Pueblo V Period.

The areal distribution of fluteplayer images, whether in rock art, on pottery, or in kiva murals, corresponds essentially to the Anasazi culture region, and includes, to a much lesser extent, the Mogollon, Hohokam, and Fremont culture areas (Fig. 1).

*Figure 34
Pictographs,
Canyon del Muerto,
Arizona.*

Over the years, fluteplayer portrayals changed considerably. For instance, earlier depictions were usually neither phallic nor humpbacked (Figs. 34 and A-5; see Fig. 8 [page 19]); head appendages (feathers, antennas, rabbit ears, etc.) appeared mainly in later periods. There were often regional cultural variations in style and concept (phallic versus nonphallic, humpbacked versus straight-backed, recumbent versus upright depictions), as well as regional tendencies emphasizing fluteplayer images in ceramics as opposed to rock art, especially in the Hohokam area.

In this section will be described the regional variations and frequency of occurrence of fluteplayer rock art images, commencing in New Mexico, moving clockwise through the Anasazi culture region of the other Four Corners states, and followed by the Fremont, Mogollon, and Hohokam culture areas.

Anasazi Area

New Mexico

In the authors' site survey, the majority of fluteplayer rock art depictions were found in the Anasazi region of New Mexico, primarily in canyons, on mesa tops, and along rivers, where habitation sites were located.

The Anasazi ("Ancient Ones" in Navajo) were primarily farmers who occupied a broad area extending from the southeastern corner of Nevada east to the Pecos River in New Mexico, and from the northern Colorado Plateau south to the mid-Rio Grande Valley (see Fig. 1). The first Anasazi rock art occurred in the Basketmaker II Period; most such rock art panels are found in habitation shelters in the canyon walls. Around A.D. 700 pottery was introduced, and various horticultural advances were made, resulting in more stable settlement patterns. These changes mark the commencement of the Pueblo phases of Anasazi culture (see Fig. 2). Most present-day Pueblo peoples are recognized as descendants of the Anasazi.

Many Anasazi rock art panels in north-central New Mexico (extending west as far as Zuni) are of the Rio Grande Style (A.D. 1350 to A.D. 1680, Pueblo IV). According to Polly Schaafsma, "The style is notable for its variety of subject matter" [rectangular anthropomorphs with exaggerated extremities, shield bearers, a wide range of fluteplayer types, masks, mammals, snakes, birds, four-pointed stars, cloud terraces] and the unending creativity displayed in the form of each figure."[2] The appearance of shields and shield bearers in Anasazi rock art may indicate Fremont influence.

The prime fluteplayer site in New Mexico is near La Cieneguilla ("Little Marsh"), a small village southwest of Santa Fe. Here the local church rests upon the ruins of the Keres pueblo of Tziguma (Pueblo IV). Kokopelli was evidently of great importance here, as he is portrayed in many different contexts: with snakes as in Figure 35 (the horned serpent was also

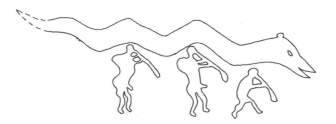

Figure 35
Petroglyph panel:
fluteplayer with snake
(Awanyu?),
La Cieneguilla,
New Mexico.
After Renaud, 1948.

*Figure 36
Petroglyph: phallic
fluteplayer with female,
La Cieneguilla,
New Mexico*

*Figure 37
Petroglyph: fluteplayer
with "cloud terrace"
legs, La Cieneguilla,
New Mexico.*

*Figure 38
Petroglyph panel:
Kokopelli with
branched flute,
La Cieneguilla,
New Mexico.*

associated with water sources and the bringing of rain); with maidens in various sexual attitudes (Fig. 36); with terrace-shaped legs in his role as rain deity (Fig. 37); with archers (also usually phallic) in his function as hunting/fertility deity (see Fig. 14 [page 22]); and with a small figure on his hump. (see Fig. 23 [page 28]). On two panels, rows of dots appear near fluteplayers; these perhaps represent raindrops, records of cyclic phenomena such as lunar periods, or merely a type of decoration (Fig. 38).

Another lively Kokopelli at this site is depicted running toward a shalako (?) figure (Fig. 39). The Zuni Shalako kachinas are important participants in the "Coming of the Gods" ceremony near the winter solstice; there is also a Hopi Shalako. Several rock art depictions of shalakos also occur in the Galisteo Basin. In addition to the usual role of kachinas in bringing rain and well-being to the people, this kachina also has a warrior/guardian aspect. At La

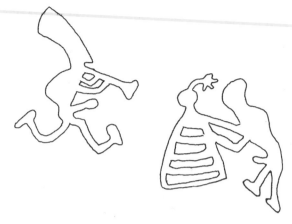

Figure 39
Petroglyph panel:
running fluteplayer
with shalako-type
figure,
La Cieneguilla,
New Mexico.

Cieneguilla Kokopelli is nearly always shown in his usual humpbacked, phallic form. Additional Kokopelli depictions from this extensive site are shown in Color Plate 2, Figure 40, Figures 21-A and 21-B, and in the Appendix (A-6, A-7, A-8, A-9, A-10, A-11, A-12, A-13, A-14, A-15, A-16, A-17, A-18, A-19, A-20, A-21, A-22, A-23, A-24, A-25, A-26, A-27, A-28, A-29, A-30).

Figure 40
Petroglyph panel:
fluteplayer with bird
and paw print,
La Cieneguilla,
New Mexico.

Not far from the nearby village of La Cienega, several fluteplayer portrayals are found. On one panel an animated figure holds his flute at an unusually high angle (Fig. 41), as if it were a trumpet. The author Carol Patterson-Rudolph claims that this particular fluteplayer is a character in the Tewa Water Jar Boy myth and that the myth as a whole is depicted on the panel (see Section v, Fig. 195 [page 133]).[3] On this and other nearby panels, a line of Kokopellis is depicted in what may be a ritual dance; another (Fig. 42) is shown with cloud terraces (as

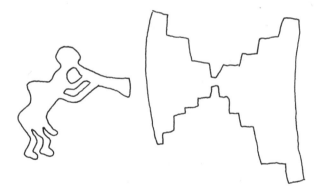

Cloud Blower?);[4] and a third is adjacent to a depiction of a member of the Arrow Swallowers, a subdivision of the Pueblo warrior societies[5] (Fig. 43).

The Arrow or Stick Swallowers (called *Nasotan* at Hopi) were participants in rituals designed to influence the weather. Arrow (or stick) swallowing was considered to be a manifestation of shamanic power but could sometimes result in death. An emetic was normally used to expel the stick or arrow at the conclusion of the ritual.[6] Snake swallowing was perhaps the ritual prototype for arrow or stick swallowing.

*Figure 43
Petroglyph panel:
fluteplayer with
Arrow Swallower,
near La Cienega,
New Mexico.*

*Figure 44
Petroglyph, La Bajada
Mesa, New Mexico.*

Several fluteplayer images occur on the slopes of La Bajada Mesa southwest of Santa Fe, one of which appears to have a third arm growing from his hump (Fig. 44). Other portrayals at this site are of a hump-backed, phallic fluteplayer (Fig. A-31) and one which is bent sharply over (Fig. 45).

Many fine Pueblo IV rock art sites are found in the Galisteo Basin near Southern Tewa pueblo ruins;

*Figure 45
Petroglyph, La Bajada
Mesa, New Mexico.*

they are distributed along miles of volcanic dikes and on cliff faces or boulders. In the rock art of the basin are numerous fluteplayers in various contexts. One of the most impressive petroglyph images is a rabbit-eared, phallic fluteplayer (Fig. 46). Nearby is a slender figure playing a very long flute, in association with a snake and bird (Fig. 47). Several insectiform and zoomorphic fluteplayer depictions also occur in the area (Figs. A-32 and A-33), as well as one figure

*Figure 46
Petroglyph panel:
"rabbit-earred," phallic
fluteplayer,
Galisteo Basin,
New Mexico.
Photo by Jeff Nelson.*

(Fig. A-34) in association with a serpent (rain-bring-ing context). One panel depicts a reclining fluteplayer in sexual union with a female figure (Fig. 48); another portrays an anthropomorph holding a long object at a high angle and facing a sun emblem or shield (Fig. A-35). This is probably not a fluteplayer but a member of the arrow- or stick-swallowing order.[7] One of the finest insectiform fluteplayer images in the basin was badly damaged by vandals attempting to remove a section of the panel (see Fig. 4 [page 12]). A site located on an isolated hill (probably a shrine) has several fluteplayers, among which is a humpbacked, phallic figure playing for a group of three slender anthropomorphs (Fig. 49). Another group of petroglyph panels in the basin shows fluteplayers with numerous birds, arrow swallowers, and other anthropomorphs (Figs. 50, 51, and 52). Other examples of fluteplayers from sites in the Gal-isteo Basin are shown in Figure 53 and in the Appen-dix (Figs. A-36, A-37, A-38, A-39, A-40, A-41, A-42, A-43, A-44, A-45, A-46, A-47, A-48, and A-49).

Figure 47 (above)
Petroglyph panel:
fluteplayer with
snake and bird,
Galisteo Basin,
New Mexico.

Figure 48
Petroglyph panel:
fluteplayer with female,
Galisteo Basin,
New Mexico.

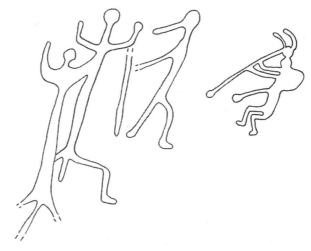

*Figure 49
Petroglyph panel:
phallic, humpbacked
fluteplayer with
anthropomorphs,
Galisteo Basin,
New Mexico.*

*Figure 50
Petroglyph panel:
fluteplayers with birds
and Arrow Swallowers,
Galisteo Basin,
New Mexico.*

Figure 51
Petroglyph panel:
fluteplayers with
birds and quadrupeds,
Galisteo Basin,
New Mexico.

Figure 52
Petroglyph panel:
fluteplayers with birds,
Galisteo Basin,
New Mexico.

*Figure 53
Petroglyph panel:
fluteplayer with turkey
tracks and snakelike
elements,
Galisteo Basin,
New Mexico.*

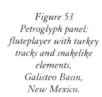

Petroglyph National Monument on the West Mesa, Albuquerque, is home to a multitude of rock art images. Seventeen thousand petroglyphs are estimated to occur here, including several fluteplayers, one with enormous feet (Fig. 54), one wearing a "kilt" and necklace (Fig. 55), another which is phallic but not humpbacked (Fig. A-50), and a fourth panel depicting three humpbacked fluteplayers (Fig. A-151). See also Figs. A-52, A-53, 56, and 57.

Figure 54
Petroglyph panel:
phallic, humpbackeed
fluteplayer with
exaggerated feet,
West Mesa,
Albuquerque,
New Mexico.

Southwest of Santa Fe, at a Tonque Arroyo site
(Pueblo IV, there are several petroglyph depictions
(Fig. 58) showing fluteplayers seated on cloud terraces (rain-bringing context). On a small mesa northeast of Isleta Pueblo, a petroglyph panel contained a
fluteplayer image, now destroyed by road building
(Fig. 59). Several fluteplayer petroglyphs are reported
at Tomé Hill, east of Los Lunas (Figs. A-54, A-55, A-
56, and A-57).

*Figure 56
Petroglyph panel:
fluteplayers with armed
figure, West Mesa,
Albuquerque,
New Mexico.*

*Figure 55
Petroglyph: fluteplayer
wearing kilt, West
Mesa, Albuquerque,
New Mexico.*

*Figure 57
Petroglyph panel:
fluteplayers with snake
and other elements,
West Mesa,
Albuquerque,
New Mexico.*

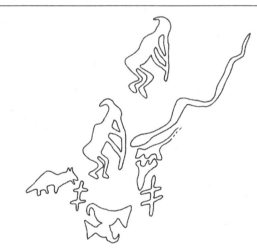

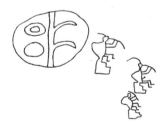

*Figure 58
Petroglyph panel: fluteplayers seated on
cloud terraces or altars,
Tonque Arroyo, New Mexico.
After Wellmann, 1979.*

*Figure 59
Petroglyph panel: fluteplayer with bird and other elements,
near Isleta Pueblo, New Mexico.
After Durham, 1955.*

Near the Tenabó Ruin (Tompiro/Pueblo IV), southwest of Mountainair on a high cliff face, is a large
panel which includes a fluteplayer (Fig. 60) near a
snake. Three other Kokopelli images were found at
or near this site (Figs. A-58, A-59, and 61). The rock
art of the Tompiro district was heavily influenced by
Jornada motifs from the south.[8] The Tompiro (or
Mountain Piro) district was a southern Rio Grande
Pueblo area located east of the river.

*Figure 60
Petroglyph panel,
Tenabó,
New Mexico.*

*Figure 61
Petroglyphs:
fluteplayers with birds,
Tenabó, New Mexico.*

Figure 62
Petroglyph panel:
fluteplayer with
carnivore track, bird,
and cloud terrace,
Cerro Indio,
New Mexico.

Figure 63
Petroglyph panel:
fluteplayer in
ritual procession,
Cerro Indio,
New Mexico.
After Marshall and
Walt, 1984.

Farther south, on a small mesa west of the Rio Grande near a Tompiro/Pueblo IV ruin, is a fluteplayer in an interesting context. He is depicted in a sitting position beneath a carnivore track, bird, and cloud terrace, and is neither humpbacked nor phallic (Fig. 62). An unusual petroglyph panel at the same site shows a humpbacked fluteplayer apparently walking in a ritual procession with a "drum major-type" personage, a second humpbacked figure, and another who appears to be bearing a large, seedlike object (Fig. 63). Another nonphallic fluteplayer was located at Hidden Mountain, west of Los Lunas (Fig. A-60).

North of Santa Fe, a humpbacked, phallic fluteplayer was found near Chamita (Fig. A-61); he plays an unusually long flute and is associated with a horned serpent. Several miles farther north, north of Española, is a major petroglyph site along the Rio

Grande. At this site are numerous fluteplayers resembling insects and animals (Figs. 64, 65, A-62, and A-63), some depicted with snakes and shields (Figs. 66 and 67), and one showing a Kokopelli-type figure pursuing a female (Fig. A-64). Others from this site are shown in Figure 68, Color Plate 7, and in the

Figure 64
Petroglyph,
north of Española,
New Mexico.

Appendix (Figs. A-65, A-66, A-67, A-68, A-69, A-70, A-71, and A-72).

In the Jemez Mountains northwest of Santa Fe, there are numerous rock art sites, most panels appearing on volcanic ash (tuff) cliffs or basalt rock surfaces. One fascinating site is Cave Kiva, located in a canyon near Los Alamos, where a number of images have been scratched through the smoke-

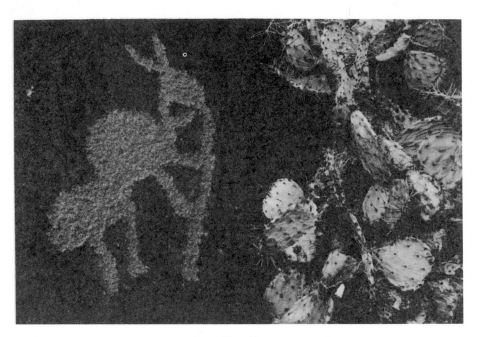

Figure 65
Petroglyph: insectiform fluteplayer, north of Española, New Mexico.

Figure 66
Petroglyph panel:
phallic, humpbacked fluteplayer with shield,
north of Española, New Mexico.

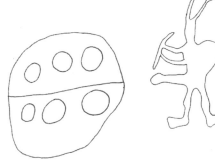

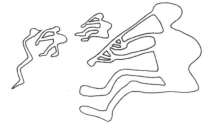

Figure 67
Petroglyph panel:
fluteplayers with snake,
north of Española, New Mexico.

Figure 68
Petroglyph panel:
fluteplayer with bird,
north of Española,
New Mexico.

blackened roof and walls into the lighter colored tuff. Here we find a "dancing" Kokopelli facing a figure with a war club who is apparently threatening an adjacent Arrow-Swallower figure;[9] there is a horned serpent to the left of the fluteplayer (Fig. 69). A tuff cliff face on Holiday Mesa (west of Jemez Springs) contains several Kokopelli depictions, the most interesting of which appears to illustrate the Hopi myth involving the unusual but successful courtship of a beautiful, unwilling maiden by Kokopelli (see Section V). As described in the myth and illustrated on this panel, Kokopelli's phallus is connected by a long, hollow reed (extending around a corner of the cliff face) to the maiden's vagina (see Fig. 193 [page 130]).

There appears to be a second depiction of the same myth nearby, but it is much smaller and less distinct (Fig. A-73). A third Kokopelli at the site is

Figure 69
Petroglyphs: fluteplayer
with Arrow Swallower,
snake, and armed
figure, Cave Kiva,
near Los Alamos,
New Mexico.

Figure 70
Petroglyph panel:
fluteplayer with
pregnant deer,
Holiday Mesa,
New Mexico.

shown next to a pregnant deer image (Fig. 70). Three humpbacked fluteplayers are known from the area of San Juan Mesa east of Jemez Springs (Figs. A-74, A-75, and A-76). One of these figures is associated with a macawlike bird, and another holds a war club instead of a flute. At Tsankawi Ruin (a separate section of Bandelier National Monument) a sitting fluteplayer is carved into the tuff (Fig. A-77), and near Tovakwa Ruin (west of Jemez Springs) is a petroglyph image of an oddly shaped fluteplayer (Fig. A-78).

Also in the Jemez Mountains, eleven Kokopellis, as well as other images, are carved into the soot-blackened walls and ceiling of a small cave room (named Fluteplayer Shrine by the authors) in Los Alamos Canyon (Fig. 71). Four of these fluteplayers are grouped two on each side of a horned snake,

Figure 71
Petroglyphs: numerous
fluteplayers and other
elements at
Fluteplayer Shrine,
near Los Alamos,
New Mexico.

again demonstrating the rain-bringing power of Kokopelli. Farther along the same cliff, two more Kokopelli figures are portrayed in a reclining position (Fig. A-79), and in a nearby cave room is a single fluteplayer with a maiden (Fig. A-80). A trio of fluteplayers occurs in another smoke-blackened cave room nearby (Fig. A-81).

In the canyon below the town of White Rock, located near Los Alamos on the west side of the Rio Grande, basalt outcrops contain several unusual petroglyphs, among them an insectiform fluteplayer (Fig. A-82), a trio with a spiral design (Fig. 72), a humpbacked, phallic figure playing what resembles a corn plant (Fig. A-83), a fluteplayer with birds (Fig.

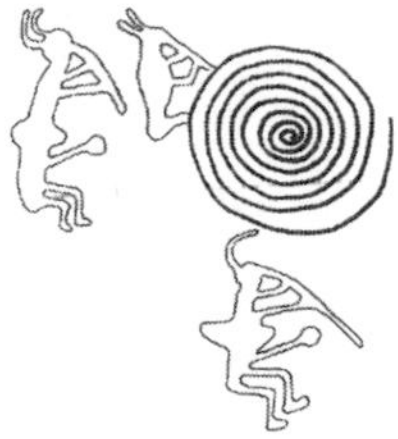

*Figure 72 (above)
Petroglyph panel: three
fluteplayers and spiral,
White Rock Canyon,
New Mexico.*

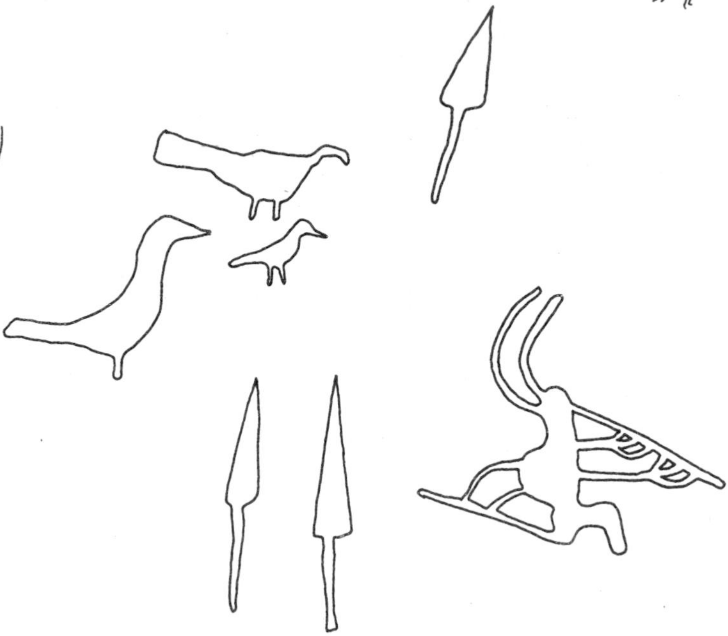

*Figure 73 (right)
Petroglyph panel:
"reversible" fluteplayer
with birds and points,
White Rock Canyon,
New Mexico.*

A-84), and what appears to be an unusual, "reversible" fluteplayer (Fig. 73). See also Figure A-85. A few miles farther north, on the east bank of the river below Otowi Bridge, a large boulder contains petroglyph images of seven fluteplayers (three of which are shown in Color Plate 3). See also Figures A-86 and A-87. In a canyon tributary to the Rio Grande, near Bandelier National Monument, is a cluster of basalt boulders on one of which is found a humpbacked fluteplayer with a female figure (Fig. 74).

*Figure 74
Petroglyph panel:
humpbacked fluteplayer
with female, near the
Rio Grande and
Bandelier National
Monument,
New Mexico. After
photo from files of
Los Alamos National
Laboratory Cultural
Resource Management
Team.*

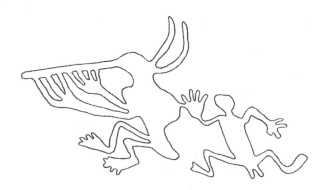

Two sitting Kokopellis, and another with an elongated, drooping hump, appear on a petroglyph panel (Fig. 75) near Cochiti Pueblo in the Rio Grande Valley. On the northern edge of the Jemez Mountains, a sandstone cliff (now submerged by the waters of Abiquiu Reservoir) was the site of a fine petroglyph panel; Kokopelli appeared there with his usual attributes—hump, phallus, and flute (Fig. A-88).

Figure 75
Petroglyph panel:
humpbacked
fluteplayers, near
Cochiti Pueblo,
New Mexico.

In the northwestern portion of New Mexico, on the banks of Navajo Lake, are a few fluteplayer panels, one of which is a Navajo pictograph (Fig. A-89); another fluteplayer panel in the area is of Pueblo origin; this petroglyph panel portrays two slender fluteplayers along with hunters and game animals (Fig. 76). A third petroglyph in this area shows an abstract fluteplayer with rows of "dancing" figures holding hands (Fig. 77). Along the San Juan River

Figure 76
Petroglyph panel:
fluteplayers with
zoomorphs, archer,
and spiral,
Navajo Lake,
New Mexico.
After Schaafsma, 1963.

Figure 77
Petroglyph panel:
stylized fluteplayer
with row of "dancers,"
Navajo Lake,
New Mexico.
After Schaafsma, 1963.

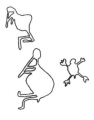

Figure 78
Petroglyph panel:
humbacked
fluteplayers with
anthropomorph (?),
near Farmington,
New Mexico.
After Smith, 1974.

near Farmington, there is a sitting, humpbacked fluteplayer with crossed legs at one site (Fig. A-90), and two other fluteplayer figures with rotund bodies at a second site (Fig. 78). In the same area, another Kokopelli with a very long flute (Fig. A-91) is depicted next to an oddly shaped anthropomorph (perhaps a birth scene), and a willowy humpbacked fluteplayer with froglike legs is portrayed nearby (Fig. A-92). This site also contains an unusual petroglyph depicting a phallic, humpbacked fluteplayer with a wavy tail, surrounded by a pecked rectangular "frame" (Fig. A-93), and another panel with four slender fluteplayers (Fig. 79).

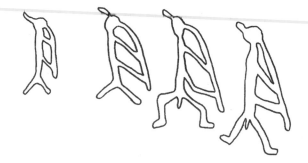

Figure 79
Petroglyphs: row of
four fluteplayers,
near Farmington,
New Mexico.

The Largo Canyon drainage, east of the above sites, boasts a large number of rock art panels, including several depictions of Ghanaskidi, the Navajo humpbacked supernatural who carries mist and seeds of all plants in his hump (see Fig. 27 and Section II, page 31). This deity may have derived from the Pueblo Kokopelli cult.[10] Ghanaskidi appears to be similarly concerned with moisture and fertility, although he never appears in the phallic mode. Pueblo IV prototypes evidently influenced seventeenth- and eighteenth-century Navajo rock art insofar as subject matter and stylistic features are concerned.[11] Other Anasazi depictions in this area include two fluteplayers joined at the head, one upside down (Fig. 80); a pictograph of two parrotlike fluteplayers back to back (Fig. 81); and two petroglyph panels in which fluteplayers seem to be playing tunes for lines of dancers (Figs. 82 and 83). None of the above is phallic.

At a site east of the Chuska Mountains and south of Shiprock, New Mexico, a zoomorphic fluteplayer is depicted next to a large, phallic anthropomorph, to the right of which is a simple, reclining fluteplayer (Color Plate 4). The scene is perhaps meant to portray the male aspect of fertility.[12] Another panel at the same site shows two Kokopellis (Fig. 84), one facing

Figure 80
Petroglyph: two
fluteplayers (one upside
down), Largo Canyon
drainage, New Mexico.
After Smith, 1974.

Figure 81
Pictograph: two
fluteplayers back to
back, Largo Canyon
drainage, New Mexico.
After Smith, 1974.

Figure 82
Petroglyph panel:
fluteplayer with row of
dancers, Largo Canyon
drainage, New Mexico.
After Smith, 1974.

Figure 83 (left)
Petroglyph panel:
fluteplayers with two
rows of dancers,
Animas Valley,
New Mexico.
After Smith, 1974.

Figure 84 (right)
Petroglyph panel:
two Kokopellis with
deer, east of the
Chuska Mountains,
New Mexico.

Figure 85
Petroglyph, east of the
Chuska Mountains,
New Mexico.

downward and "hovering" over the other, both surrounded by deer (hunting-magic context). A third depiction at this site is of a big-footed fluteplayer with a three-feathered headdress (Fig. 85).

The Chaco Canyon area and Chaco Culture National Historic Park, in New Mexico, are home to a multitude of fine rock art panels. One of the most impressive sites contains seventeen fluteplayers in two adjacent panels, one of which depicts ten phallic fluteplayers associated with what may possibly be two birth scenes (six fluteplayers and a "birth scene" are shown in Figure 86). At this site are some very unusual fluteplayers with exaggerated feet and knobby knees (Figs. 87 and A-94). Feet seem to be of special importance here and are portrayed frequently and prominently on one of the panels (Fig. 88).

Figure 86
Petroglyph panel:
six fluteplayers and
"birth scene,"
Chaco Canyon
area,
New Mexico.

Figure 87
Petroglyphs:
fluteplayers and
paw prints,
Chaco Canyon area,
New Mexico.

At another Chaco Canyon site, Fluteplayer Rock, are depicted six Kokopellis (all humpbacked and nonphallic) in a context of animals, birds, and handprints (Fig. 89). One of these humpbacked flute-players, with elaborate head appendages, is next to a doglike zoomorph.

Figure 88
Petroglyph panel:
humpbacked, phallic
fluteplayer with goat
and paw prints,
Chaco Canyon area,
New Mexico.

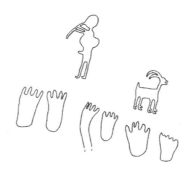

*Figure 89
Petroglyph panel at
Fluteplayer Rock:
humpbacked
fluteplayers with
zoomorphs, birds, and
hand prints,
Chaco Canyon,
New Mexico.
After file photo from
National Park Service.*

Several other flute-players are depicted at Chaco Canyon: two sitting fluteplayers facing each other on either side of a spiral or snake (Fig. A-95); a recumbent Kokopelli above a snake (Fig. A-96); a procession of fourteen stick-figure fluteplayers (Fig. 90); three "bowlegged" fluteplayers with adjacent snakes (Fig. 91); a humpbacked Kokopelli with a large abdominal protrusion (Fig. 92); two fluteplayers with

Figure 90
Petroglyph panel:
fluteplayer procession,
Chaco Canyon,
New Mexico.
After file photo from
National Park Service.

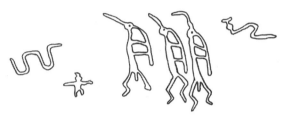

Figure 91
Petroglyph panel:
fluteplayers with snakes
and anthropomorph,
Chaco Canyon,
New Mexico.
After file photo from
National Park Service.

very large feet, one of the former in a context of animals and small anthropomorphs (Fig. 93); and various other humpbacked fluteplayers (Figs. A-97, A-98, and Fig. 94).

In a canyon tributary to the Rio Puerco, southeast of Cuba, New Mexico, several petroglyph panels depict fluteplayers (Fig. 95 and Figs. A-99, A-100). There are also two depictions of twinned fluteplayers sitting back-to-back (Fig. A-101 and Fig. 96), and reclining figures associated with spirals and other designs (Fig. 97).

East of Gallup, New Mexico, several simple fluteplayers (two reclining and one standing) appear on a petroglyph panel together with stick-figure anthropomorphs (Fig. 98). On the opposite wall of the same small canyon is an interesting petroglyph panel (probably historic) portraying a small fluteplayer, a simple anthropomorph (lizard-man?), a Zia sun-symbol with mask, and a cloud element with rain (Fig. 99).

Figure 92
Petroglyph, Chaco
Canyon, New Mexico.
After Steed, 1980.

Figure 93
Petroglyph panel:
humpbacked fluteplayer
with zoomorph and
anthropomorphs,
Chaco Canyon,
New Mexico.

Figure 94 (above)
Petroglyph:
humpbacked fluteplayer,
Chaco Canyon,
New Mexico.

Figure 95 (left)
Petroglyph panel:
recumbent fluteplayer
with unusual design,
Tapia Canyon,
New Mexico.

Figure 96
Petroglyph panel:
twinned fluteplayers
with blanket (?) design,
Tapia Canyon,
New Mexico.

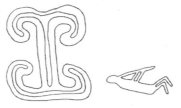

Figure 97 (left)
Petroglyph panel:
recumbent fluteplayer
with spirals,
Tapia Canyon,
New Mexico.

Figure 98 (right)
Petroglyphs, east of
Gallup, New Mexico.

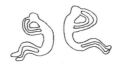

Farther south, near Zuni Pueblo, are numerous panels, one with two humpbacked fluteplayers (Fig. 100), one depicting a fluteplayer with mountain goats and snakes (Fig. 101), and a third showing a fluteplayer (see Fig. 12 [page 21]) with stylized animals or insects. At Zuni the fluteplayer is called Chu'lu'laneh, which is also the name for the type of

Figure 99 (above) Petroglyph panel: fluteplayer with sun-symbol mask,anthropomorph, and cloud element, east of Gallup, New Mexico.

Figure 100 (above) Petroglyphs: humpbacked fluteplayers, Zuni Reservation, New Mexico.

Figure 101 (left) Petroglyph panel: fluteplayer with bighorn sheep and snakes, Zuni Reservation, New Mexico. Photo by Jeff Nelson.

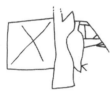

flute used by the rain priests. Paiyatamu is a flute-playing Zuni mythological character but is not humpbacked (see Section V).[13] See also Figures 102 and 103 and A-102 and A-103.

Close to the southern boundary of the Anasazi culture area near Quemado, New Mexico, a petroglyph panel portrays a dancing (or sitting) fluteplayer (see Fig. 22 [page 27]) in a context of hand prints, footprints, snakes, and animals. A few miles farther south, two fluteplayers are pecked on sandstone cliffs, one depicting a small, phallic fluteplayer with a curled head appendage and tail (Fig. A-104). A few feet away, a phallic fluteplayer (also with a curled head appendage) is shown next to a female figure holding one hand to her abdomen (Fig. 104), in negative pecking technique suggesting an empty womb and possible birth scene (fertility context).

Arizona

Westward in the Anasazi area of Arizona are the sites at Hardscrabble Wash, southeast of Holbrook, in a sparsely populated area not far from the New Mexico state line. This is a major petroglyph site (Basketmaker II to the present) having cultural and mythological links to Zuni,[14] a few miles farther east. Rock art style and content are quite similar to that at Zuni; fluteplayer depictions in the wash appear to occur from Basketmaker III into Pueblo III. The Rio Grande Style began to influence Zuni-Cibola/Hardscrabble Wash area rock art about A.D. 1325.[15]

A panel near the head of the canyon portrays a seated Kokopelli in a context of masks and insects (Fig. 105). Lines of "dancing" stick figures and several snakes accompany a fluteplayer on another panel (Fig. 106). A cliff face in the wash is crowded with images of anthropomorphs in great variety—snakes, animal tracks, and many other elements. In the midst of these numerous images, a zoomorphic fluteplayer might be viewed as trying to bring order to chaos through his melodies (Fig. 107). Insectiform and

Figure 105
Petroglyph panel: seated Kokopelli with masks and insects or zoomorphs, Hardscrabble Wash, Arizona. After Young, 1988.

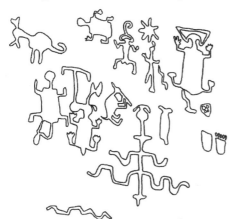

Figure 106 (above)
Petroglyph panel: fluteplayer with snakes and row of dancers, Hardscrabble Wash, Arizona. After Young, 1988.

Figure 107 (left)
Petroglyph panel: insectiform fluteplayer with anthropomorphs, zoomorphs, and snakelike elements, Hardscrabble Wash, Arizona. After Young, 1988.

Figure 108 (above, left)
Petroglyph: fluteplayer
with double hump,
Hardscrabble Wash,
Arizona.

humpbacked fluteplayers are depicted on other panels at the same site (Figs. 108, 109, and 110 and Fig.
A-105).

Figure 109 (above, right)
Petroglyph: phallic,
humpbacked fluteplayer
with forked head
appendages,
Hardscrabble Wash,
Arizona.

Within Canyon de Chelly National Monument
(Canyon de Chelly, and its tributary Canyon del
Muerto) the high-walled canyons contain a wealth of
rock art. Approximately two hundred sites are

Figure 110 (right)
Petroglyph panel: seated
fluteplayers with
triangular humps,
Hardscrabble Wash,
Arizona.

known. Pictographic panels predominate (about three-fourths of total representations),[16] the primary reason being that the canyon walls are so high that the desert-varnish patination required for creating petroglyphs rarely reaches the canyon floor.[17] The pictograph panels are usually found in association with ruins in protected rock shelters and alcoves. This rock art dates from Basketmaker II through modern Navajo;[18] the many fluteplayer panels in the monument can be assigned a date range extending from Basketmaker III into Pueblo III.

One early petroglyph panel (Pueblo I) in the Tunnel Canyon tributary shows two "sitting" fluteplayers, one perched on the head of a man (Fig. A-106). On another petroglyph panel from the early period, the stick-figure fluteplayer's instrument appears to be a combined atlatl and flute (Fig. 111). The atlatl was an early hunting aid, preceding the bow and arrow; it extended the human arm by an extra wooden "joint," thus helping the hunter to propel the dart with greater force. Many pictograph fluteplayer portrayals also date from the early period, during which time twinned figures were common. Two such depictions were done in white pigment (Figs. 112 and 113), and a third in red and white. The latter panel shows two fluteplayers (Color Plate 5), each seated under a "rainbow" element (rain deity context?).

During the Pueblo III Period, petroglyphs, in Canyon de Chelly at least, were produced by a shallower pecking technique than previously;[19] most petroglyph panels in the canyon belong to this period and to late Pueblo II.[20] Fluteplayer portrayals on panels of this period include one in which the subject is an elongated stick figure with a hump and a bird's

Figure 111
Petroglyph: Canyon de Chelly, Arizona. After Grant, 1978

Figure 112
Petroglyph: Canyon de Chelly, Arizona. After Grant, 1978.

Figure 113
Petroglyph: Canyon de Chelly, Arizona. After Grant, 1978.

Figure 114
Petroglyph: hump-
backed fluteplayer with
bird's head, Canyon de
Chelly, Arizona.
After Grant, 1978.

Figure 115
Petroglyph: hump-
backed, bird-headed
fluteplayer, east of
Petrified Forest
National Park,
Arizona.
After Grant, 1978.

Figure 116
Petroglyph: bird-headed
fluteplayer,
near Moab, Utah.
After Warner, 1989.

head (Fig. 114). The latter feature may be related to the shamanistic capability of magical "soul-flight."[21] A similar figure (Fig. 115) is found just east of Petrified Forest National Park, in Arizona, and another near Moab, Utah (Fig 116). Other petroglyph panels of the period depict "seated," stick-figure fluteplayers with long instruments (Figs. A-107 and A-108), twinned fluteplayers with feather head elements (Fig. 117), and fluteplayers playing a common instrument connecting the two figures (Fig. 118).

Two other unusual Pueblo III petroglyph panels in Canyon de Chelly are located near Sleeping Duck Ruin. One of these contains numerous elements, including six fluteplayers in a variety of poses (recumbent, twinned [Fig. 119], bird-headed), anthropomorphs, and several types of animals. On another panel at this site, two Kokopellis are flanked by a snake, a figure with a planting stick (see Fig. 19 [page 24]), a bird-headed man, two other planting sticks, and what may represent a sprouting seed.

Pictograph panels from the Pueblo III sites in the Canyon de Chelly National Monument can be distinguished from earlier representations by inferior style and technique. The primary reason for this change is that ritual artistic endeavors were more and more confined to kivas and the mural paintings therein, rock art becoming increasingly concerned with portrayals of everyday life.[22] Several Pueblo III pictographs from the monument are presented in this book: one, in Many Cherry Canyon tributary, portrays an extremely phallic Kokopelli (Fig. A-109) next to crudely painted animals and anthropomorphs; another, in Fluteplayer Cave, depicts a reclining, humpbacked fluteplayer (Color Plate 6). Similar figures are found at Ledge Ruin and Cable Cave (Figs. A-110 and A-111). A row of three fluteplayers painted in white pigment is portrayed on a panel in Canyon del Muerto (see Fig. 34).

Petrified Forest National Park straddles Interstate 40 east of Holbrook, Arizona. Within the park are numerous petroglyph panels, mostly in the Puerco Ruin area. One fluteplayer depiction at this site (late Pueblo II to Pueblo III) is of the phallic, bigfooted type, appearing next to a small anthropomorph and a row of dots (Color Plate 8). On another panel in the park, a fluteplayer is depicted in a row of animals and birds above a female anthropomorph (Fig. 120). Just east of the park boundary, a reclining fluteplayer is portrayed on a petroglyph panel (Fig. A-112); his arms and flute are executed in a scratching technique, whereas the rest of his body is pecked into the rock surface. Preliminary designs were probably often scratched on the rock prior to completion by pecking and/or incision techniques. At a petroglyph site on the Rio Puerco east of the park are two fluteplayers: a sitting figure with "cloven hooves"

Figure 117
Petroglyphs: twinned fluteplayers, Canyon de Chelly, Arizona. After Grant, 1978.

Figure 118
Petroglyphs: twinned fluteplayers, Canyon de Chelly, Arizona. After Grant, 1978.

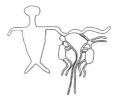

Figure 119 (above) Petroglyphs: twinned fluteplayers with anthropomorph, Canyon de Chelly, Arizona. After Grant, 1978.

Figure 120 (left) Petroglyph panel: fluteplayer with female, birds, and animals, Petrified Forest National Park, Arizona. After Patterson, 1992.

Figure 121
Petroglyph panel:
seated fluteplayer and
anthropomorph
connected to snake, east
of Petrified Forest
National Park,
Arizona.

next to a big-footed figure with a snake on his arm (Fig. 121), and a bird-headed fluteplayer (see Figure 115 [page 72]).

Farther west, near Holbrook, is a series of late Anasazi petroglyph panels on a sandstone cliff and boulders. The iconography displayed on the escarpment panel includes a large-footed, stick-figure fluteplayer (Fig. A-5) surrounded by bear tracks and game animals. There also appear to be Archaic/Basketmaker panels at this site.

Western Archaic rock art is the oldest in the Southwest, commencing around 5500 B.C. , and was made by hunter-gatherers who lived in small groups and moved between seasonal camps. The earliest Western Archaic rock art was abstract, followed later by the addition of zoomorphic and anthropomorphic elements in both petroglyph and pictograph form. The ideography of their rock art was heavily influenced by shamanism.

The shaman was a priest-healer who was believed to possess supernatural or psychic powers received through trances and dreams, frequently achieved by the use of hallucinogens. He or she was responsible for healing the sick, revealing the arcane, and using his power to control events that affected the fertility of crops, game animals, and the tribe itself. Bird symbolism was important in shamanism, thence the concept of magical "soul-flight." Shamans used masks to give tangible form to the power of their relationship to their spirit helpers (in contexts of magical "soul-flight," hunting magic, healing, etc.). They evidently chose to represent themselves in rock art in order to fix their power in concrete expression. Shamans sometimes impersonated kachinas; horns on human figures shown with fluteplayers probably indicate their shamanic powers (Fig. 122).

Several fluteplayers can be found at three neighboring petroglyph sites south of Holbrook, in canyons near the headwaters of the Little Colorado. On one panel, two phallic fluteplayers are depicted, one behind the other (Fig. 123); another panel shows a fluteplayer apparently wearing a belt or sash (Fig. 124); and the third portrays a rare example of the fluteplayer in frontal view holding his flute upwards (see Color Plate 1). This figure is adjacent to what appears to be a bird (macaw?) with a tether around its neck, or sitting in a hoop. At the same site, another petroglyph panel depicts a fluteplayer unusual in his being connected to amorphous figures and a zoomorph (Fig. A-113). Fluteplayers are shown with other anthropomorphs on panels at nearby sites (Figs. 125, 126 and Figs. A-114, A-115).

A few miles southwest of Holbrook, a canyon site containing mainly Basketmaker rock art includes two repatinated "backpacker" figures with walking

Figure 122
Petroglyph: fluteplayer
joined to horn of
anthropomorph
(probably a shaman),
Capitol Reef National
Park, Utah.
After Warner, 1990.

Figure 123 (below)
Petroglyphs:
two phallic fluteplayers,
south of
Holbrook, Arizona.

Figure 124 (right)
Petroglyph:
fluteplayer wearing belt
or sash, south of
Holbrook, Arizona.

Figure 125 (below)
Petroglyph panel:
fluteplayers and
anthropomorphs,
south of
Holbrook, Arizona.

*Figure 126
Petroglyph panel:
fluteplayer with
animal and
anthropomorphs, south
of Holbrook, Arizona.*

sticks (Fig. A-116) and a slender figure with a bird on its head that was presumably a fluteplayer, but over which a snake image has been superimposed across the flute area (Fig. A-117). Just north of Winslow, Arizona, on a mesa escarpment at Homol'ovi State Park, a late Anasazi reclining fluteplayer is depicted below several kachina masks (Fig. 127).

In the Monument Valley area of northeastern Arizona, near an Anasazi ruin, are several late Anasazi petroglyph panels. In one scene (Fig. 128), a legless fluteplayer is depicted in the company of several bighorn sheep, one of which is being "lassoed" by

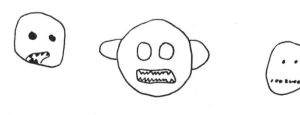

*Figure 127
Petroglyph panel:
recumbent fluteplayer
with masks,
Homol'ovi State Park,
Arizona.
After Cole, 1989b.*

a running hunter (hunting-magic context). In this
unusual, somewhat narrative scene, the hunter's
footprints are shown "running" up the panel to his
ultimate position behind the bighorn sheep; motion
is visually implied. On the opposite wall of the same
small canyon are two panels: one, evidently also
involving hunting magic, portrays another narrative
scene with a standing Kokopelli, a small, reclining
fluteplayer, as well as bighorn sheep. Animal tracks
and human footprints are other elements (Fig. 129).

*Figure 128
Petroglyph panel:
fluteplayer in hunting-
magic context,
Monument Valley,
Arizona.
After Renaud, 1948.*

*Figure 129
Petroglyph panel:
humpbacked
fluteplayers in
hunting-magic context,
Marsh Pass, Arizona.
From Kidder and
Guernsey, 1919.*

Although the actual hunters are not depicted, the
human footprints probably symbolize their presence, resulting in economy of time and effort
required to produce the complete figures. The second panel on this side of the canyon depicts four
recumbent, humpbacked fluteplayers flanking a line
of human footprints, and a fifth fluteplayer, phallic
and in a sitting or dancing position (see Fig. 24 [page
29]).

Long House Valley, west of Kayenta, is the site of
a petroglyph panel (Pueblo II/III) showing two reclining, humpbacked, insectiform fluteplayers (see Fig. 7
[page 19]) with bighorn sheep, one of which has been
pierced by an arrow. In Navajo National Monument,
between Page and Kayenta, at the Keet Seel Ruin
(Pueblo III), is a pictograph portrayal of a reclining

fluteplayer painted in gray (see Fig. 8 [page 19]). Not far away, but outside the monument, is Fluteplayer Cave, in an arm of Tsegi Canyon. Here is probably the largest fluteplayer recorded in the realm of Indian rock art; this recumbent figure is about five feet long and is painted in white clay (Fig. 130). South of Kayenta is a petroglyph panel showing four fluteplayers along with other figures in a dreamlike context (Fig. 131). From one figure's flute appears to sprout flowering vegetation or perhaps magic symbolism.

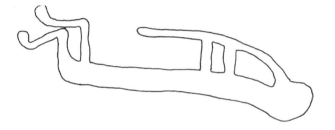

Figure 130
Pictograph:
five-foot-long,
reclining fluteplayer,
Tsegi Canyon, Arizona.
After Schaafsma, 1980.

At Walnut Canyon National Monument near Flagstaff, Arizona, a petroglyph panel depicts two zoomorphic fluteplayers facing each other, their downward-pointed flutes joined at the tips (Fig. A-118). Several miles north of this site, near Wupatki National Monument, is an interesting scene showing a recumbent fluteplayer associated with copulating animals and humans (Fig. 132). Also near the monument are a number of elaborate petroglyph panels; one early Pueblo panel portrays a row of abstract anthropomorphic figures at one end of which is a horizontal fluteplayer held aloft by an anthropomorph in a pose reminiscent of a modern-day professional wrestling match! This unusual depiction (Fig. 133) may represent a ritual honoring the fluteplayer. To the right of this element is an anthropomorph

*Figure 131
Petroglyph panel:
several fluteplayers
with anthropomorphs,
south of
Kayenta, Arizona.
After photo by
Reed Lance.*

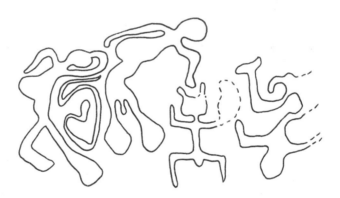

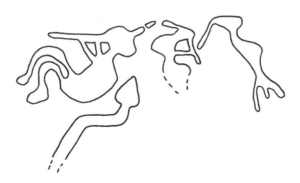

*Figure 132
Petroglyph panel:
recumbent fluteplayer
in copulation scene,
near Wupatki
National Monument,
Arizona.
After Patterson, 1992.*

*Figure 133
Petroglyph panel:
recumbent fluteplayer
held aloft by one
figure in a line of
anthropomorphs,
near Wupatki
National
Monument,
Arizona.
Photo by
David Grant Noble.*

(with earrings) extending a hand toward the "wrestling" pair. Another nearby panel depicts three fluteplayers (Fig. A-119) in a complex setting of animals, tracks, anthropomorphs, a spiral, and other elements. Several fluteplayer rock art portrayals are also found within Wupatki National Monument. Four

*Figure 134
Petroglyph panel:
seated fluteplayers with
zoomorphs,
Wupatki National
Monument, Arizona.*

*Figure 135
Petroglyph panel:
seated and recumbent
fluteplayers with birds,
snake, and other
elements, Wupatki
National Monument,
Arizona.*

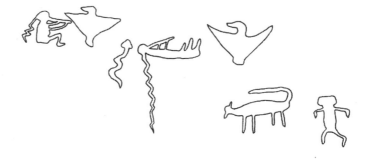

*Figure 136
Petroglyph panel:
recumbent fluteplayers
with zoomorph and
other elements,
Wupatki National
Monument, Arizona.*

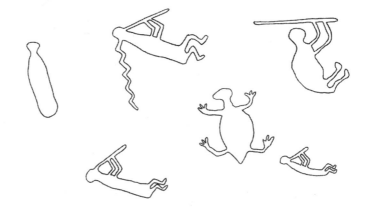

petroglyph panels near some remote ruins contain small (two- to six-inch) figures depicting reclining or sitting fluteplayers along with birds and animals (Figs. 134, 135, 136 and Fig. A-120).

Most rock art sites in the Walnut Canyon/Wupatki area are part of the Sinagua tradition, a culture on the fringes of the Western Anasazi with Mogollon and Hohokam relationships.

The Sinagua people appeared in this region in the seventh century A.D. and maintained their complex tradition until the fourteenth century, when their culture began to merge into that of the Hopi,[23] some clans of which are now considered descendants of the Sinagua. Their rock art iconography was influenced by the Anasazi to the northeast as well as by the Hohokam, from whom the Sinagua apparently adapted the beautifully executed and elaborate textile designs seen on petroglyph panels in the area.[24] Some Kayenta (Western) Anasazi sites in Wupatki National Monument also contain textile and/or pottery designs.

The westernmost fluteplayer site recorded in the Anasazi region of Arizona was in Snake Gulch, south of Fredonia. Here, on an extensive Cave Valley Style[25] pictograph panel (early Anasazi), a reclining, humpbacked fluteplayer lies at the feet of an anthropomorph composed of triangular elements (Fig. 137). Elements on Cave Valley Style panels typically consist of human figures with broad-shouldered, tapered bodies and triangular arms and legs; these are usually pictographs painted in a variety of colors. A second reclining fluteplayer, painted in red, also is recorded from Snake Gulch (Fig. A-121).

*Figure 137
Pictographs:
recumbent,
humpbacked
fluteplayer with
Cave Valley Style
anthropomorph,
Snake Gulch, Arizona.
After Schaafsma, 1980.*

Utah

Numerous fluteplayer depictions were recorded in the rock art of Utah, mostly in the eastern third of the state and primarily in the Anasazi culture area. A convenient but inexact northern boundary of this area is the Colorado River (Fig. 1); several Anasazi fluteplayer rock art sites do occur north of the river, however. North of the Snake Gulch site, across the Utah border and a few miles east of Kanab, is a petroglyph panel depicting a fluteplayer with attendant anthropomorphs (Fig. 138). A fluteplayer with head appendages and tail was recorded west of Kanab near the Arizona border (Fig. A-122); a few miles farther north, at the Cave Valley type-site, a pictograph panel apparently contains a depiction of twinned fluteplayers next to a large anthropomorph (Fig. 139). Other fluteplayers are reported from the St. George, Utah, area and from the Valley of Fire State Park near Overton, Nevada (Fig. A-123). The latter is the westernmost rock art site where fluteplayer images were recorded.

Figure 138
Petroglyphs:
fluteplayer with
anthropomorphs,
near Kanab, Utah.
After Steward, 1941.

Along the San Juan River in the southeast part of Utah are a number of outstanding San Juan Anthropomorphic Style[26] (Basketmaker II) panels. This style is characterized by large, broad-shouldered anthropomorphs in frontal attitudes, usually wearing elaborate ceremonial regalia. The type-sites for the style are near the confluence of Butler Wash and the San Juan River. At these sites are several subsequent fluteplayer depictions—one, a humpbacked type (Fig. A-124), is associated with an archer; others (Fig. 140) are shown with a large, phallic anthropomorph (fertility context?). At the same site a reclining stick-

Figure 139
Pictographs: twinned
fluteplayers with
anthropomorph,
Cave Valley, Utah.

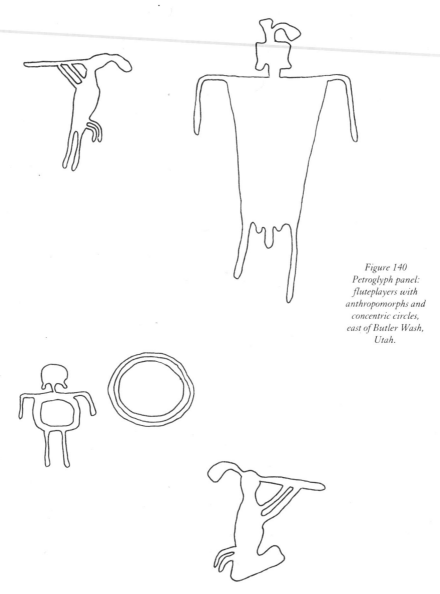

*Figure 140
Petroglyph panel:
fluteplayers with
anthropomorphs and
concentric circles,
east of Butler Wash,
Utah.*

figure fluteplayer serenades a bird-headed anthropomorph with enormous hands and feet (Fig. A-125). At
another site along the San Juan, a fluteplayer is shown
attached at the head by a long, wavy line to the tail of

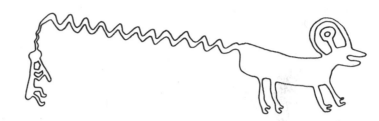

Figure 141
Petroglyphs:
seated fluteplayer
attached to tail of
bighorn sheep,
near San Juan River,
Utah.
After Warner, 1990.

Figure 142
Petroglyphs:
fluteplayers with
long head
appendages and
large feet,
San Juan River —
Butler Wash, Utah.

a bighorn sheep (Fig. 141). See also Figures 142 and 143.

A few miles up Butler Wash is a very finely pecked, San Juan Basketmaker Style petroglyph panel on which a later (?), recumbent fluteplayer is portrayed (Fig. A-126). Still farther north, high on Comb Ridge, is located the fascinating Procession Panel. Here, four lines of anthropomorphic figures (more than 150) converge at a large circle in which are two small, lobed circles. One rock art researcher believes these small circles may represent the War Twins of Pueblo mythology.[27] In one line of figures at this site, several fluteplayers can be seen, perhaps intended to provide ritual music for

Figure 143
Petroglyphs:
recumbent fluteplayer
with snake and rows
of dots,
San Juan River —
Butler Wash, Utah.

Color Plate 1 (Above):
Petroglyph panel: fluteplayer in frontal view, Fivemile Draw, Arizona.

Color Plate 2 (Below):
Petroglyph panel: Three humpbacked fluteplayers, La Cieneguilla, New Mexico.

Color Plate 3 (Above):
Petroglyph panel: three phallic, humpbacked fluteplayers, north of White Rock Canyon, New Mexico.

Color Plate 4 (Below):
Petroglyph panel: zoomorphic and recumbent fluteplayers with phallic anthropomorph, east of the Chuska Mountains, New Mexico.

Color Plate 5 (Above):
Pictograph panel: twinned fluteplayers seated under "rainbows" and large white bird, Canyon de Chelly, Arizona.

Color Plate 6 (Below):
Pictograph panel: reclining, humpbacked fluteplayer with handprints, Canyon de Chelly, Arizona.

Color Plate 7
Petroglyph:
zoomorphic fluteplayer,
near Velarde,
New Mexico.

Color Plate 8
Petroglyph panel:
phallic fluteplayer,
anthropomorph, and
row of dots,
Petrified Forest
National Park,
Arizona.

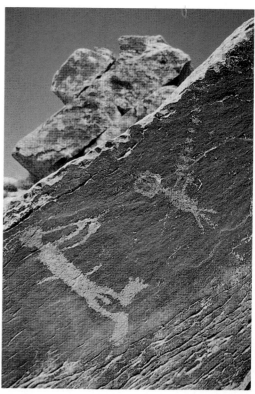

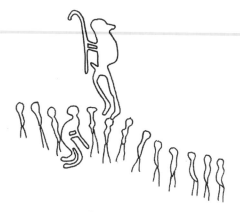

*Figure 144
Petroglyphs:
procession scene with
fluteplayer and phallic
figure with cane,
Comb Ridge, Utah.*

the procession (Fig. 144). Also depicted are several humpbacked, phallic figures holding crooks and stand-ing above the lines of people.

East of the mouth of Butler Wash there is a line of sandstone cliffs on the north bank of the San Juan; this is the Sand Island site, an extensive and well-known petroglyph area. Several different styles occur here, those of the Pueblo I through Pueblo III periods being the most pertinent to our fluteplayer survey. Many fluteplayers are depicted on these crowded panels; one is extremely phallic (Fig. 145) and is associated with game animals and anthropomorphs. On the same large panel are two other sets of fluteplayer depictions; the first portrays two phallic fluteplayers, one with a bird on his head and a horned serpent near his back (Fig. A-127); the second scene shows a phallic fluteplayer facing an odd, quasi-circular element divided into segments (Fig. A-128). Nearby is a depic-tion of the zoomorphic type—a flute-playing bighorn sheep (see Fig. 28 [page 32] and Section II, page 18). Perhaps this sort of portrayal was a type of hunting-magic shorthand in which the artist combined the flute of Kokopelli (as hunting deity) with the bighorn

*Figure 145
Petroglyph:
extremely phallic
fluteplayer with long
head appendages,
Sand Island, Utah.*

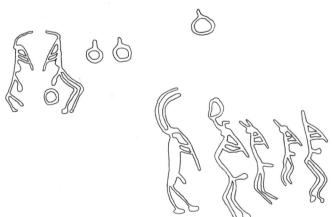

*Figure 146
Petroglyph panel:
seven phallic
fluteplayers with
lobed circles,
Sand Island, Utah.
After photo by Hugh
Crouse.*

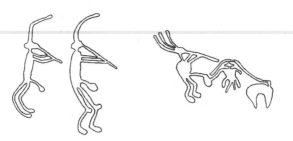

*Figure 147
Petroglyph panel:
three phallic
fluteplayers and
possible birth scene,
Sand Island, Utah.
After photo by
Hugh Crouse.*

sheep (object of the hunt); the intent was possibly the reduction of effort and time required to produce both images separately. The creation of petroglyphs can be hard work! On other panels here are shown rows of slender, phallic fluteplayers (Figs. 146 and 147) and a pair of fluteplayers seated back to back (Fig. A-129).

Near Bluff, east of Sand Island, many petroglyph panels are found on sandstone cliffs. A fluteplayer with animals is depicted on one panel (Fig. A-130; on another, two back-to-back fluteplayers are shown in nearly mirror-image sitting positions (Fig. A-131). In the same area, one interesting petroglyph panel portrays a row of figures: five fluteplayers to the right and four fluteplayers to the left of a centrally placed plant form (yucca in bloom?). All nine fluteplayers are phallic and wear an unusual variety of head-

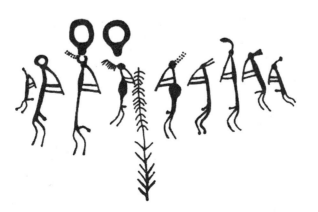

*Figure 148
Petroglyph panel:
nine phallic
fluteplayers facing
central plant form,
near Bluff, Utah.
After Manning, 1990.*

dresses; one is humpbacked (Fig. 148). In the same general region are two other panels—one depicting a phallic fluteplayer with a crook (see Fig. 33 [page 33]), another showing two phallic fluteplayers with unusual, notched headdresses (Fig. A-132). Farther upriver is a petroglyph site containing a humpbacked fluteplayer, a snake, and other anthropomorphs (Fig. A-133). See also Figures 149, 150 and Figures A-134, A-135.

In Chinle Wash, Utah, a few miles to the west, is a petroglyph panel on which a reclining and a seated fluteplayer are associated with an anthropomorph

Figure 149
Petroglyph panel:
recumbent fluteplayer
with anthropomorphs
and atlatls (?), along
San Juan River near
Bluff, Utah.

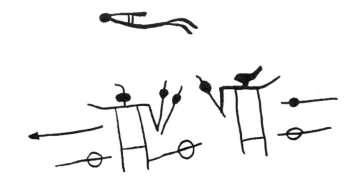

Figure 150
Petroglyph panel:
fluteplayers with
anthropomorphs and
atlatls or arrows,
along San Juan River
near Bluff, Utah.

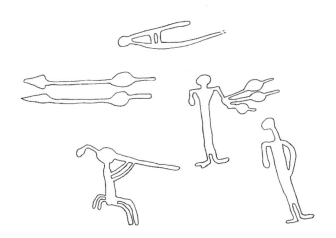

with huge, upraised hands (Fig. 151). In Montezuma Canyon, northeast of Bluff, is a petroglyph of a fluteplayer "serenading" a large bird (Fig. A-136).

Draining Cedar Mesa, south of Natural Bridges National Monument, Grand Gulch and its tributaries contain dozens of Basketmaker and Pueblo rock art sites, mostly pictographs. High in an alcove is a small fluteplayer in red pigment (Fig. A-137). Another red Kokopelli figure appears on a pictograph panel with two "arthritic," knobby-kneed old men with canes (Fig. 152).[28] These are probably Basketmaker III panels.

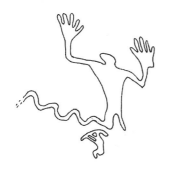

Figure 151
Petroglyph panel:
fluteplayer with
anthropomorph,
Chinle Wash, Utah.
After photo by
Polly Schaafsma.

Figure 152
Pictograph panel:
fluteplayer with
"crippled"
anthropomorphs,
Grand Gulch, Utah.
After Vuncannon, 1976.

A petroglyph in lower Grand Gulch depicts a fluteplayer in association with a snake, a lizard-man, and an anthropomorph (Fig. 153). To the south, near the mouth of Johns Canyon, a tributary of the San Juan, several early Anasazi fluteplayers are depicted

Figure 153
Petroglyph panel:
humpbacked
fluteplayer with
anthropomorph, snake,
and zoomorph (?),
Grand Gulch, Utah.
After photo from
BLM files.

on large boulders. One is an angular, reclining stick figure (Fig. A-138); another Kokopelli is shown in the company of a line of humpbacked figures and a large atlatl (Fig. 154).

The canyons of the Colorado and San Juan rivers contain numerous rock art sites, many of which have been destroyed by the rising waters of Lake Powell.

Figure 154
Petroglyph panel:
phallic fluteplayer
with row of
humpbacked figures,
atlatl, and possible
rain symbolism,
Johns Canyon, Utah.
After Vuncannon, 1978.

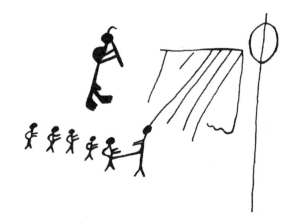

One of the finest petroglyph sites (Pueblo III) was at the mouth of Smith Fork. Among hundreds of figures at this now-submerged site were two fluteplayers, one in a reclining position adjacent to a snake and an anthropomorph with large hands (Fig. A-139).[29] Another submerged fluteplayer site was on Ticaboo Creek (Fig. A-140), and a third such site was opposite the mouth of Last Chance Canyon—a humpbacked fluteplayer near a line of humpbacked figures, spirals, and geometric designs (Fig. 155). At Trail Canyon mouth, also inun-

Figure 155
Petroglyph panel:
humpbacked
fluteplayers with
row of "backpacker"
figures and triangle
motif, Glen Canyon
area (Last Chance
Canyon), Utah.
After Foster, 1954.

dated, was a petroglyph design composed of adjoining squares, in one of which a running or dancing Kokopelli was portrayed (Fig. 156). At a submerged site in lower Cha Canyon, a stick-figure fluteplayer (Fig. A-141) was shown in a context of game animals, anthropomorphs, snakes, and a geometric design. On the same panel was a hunter stalking a bighorn sheep with bow and arrow (the fluteplayer in hunting-magic context). See also Figure A-142.

The rapid development of the Southwest, concentrated mainly in the last one hundred years of our

Figure 156
Petroglyph panel:
phallic, humpbacked
fluteplayer in
blanket (?) design,
Glen Canyon
(Trail Canyon mouth),
Utah.
After Turner, 1963.

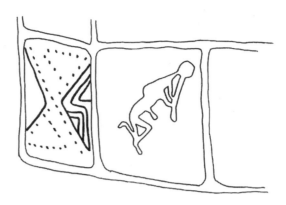

history, has resulted in the unfortunate destruction of much of our cultural heritage. The construction of railroads, highways, housing developments, and dams, as well as the extension and enlargement of agricultural areas, has destroyed much rock art and many habitation sites, shrines, and other cultural remains left by prehistoric Native Americans. Today, the federal and some state governments require an archaeological salvage study of areas subject to new construction and other types of disruption in an effort to record any evidence of prehistoric habitation at such sites. These studies also usually involve the recording and documentation of rock art panels which are to be submerged or otherwise destroyed.

In the Indian Creek drainage, northwest of Monticello, Utah, are numerous panels; four of these are early Anasazi, one of them (Fig. 157) depicting a fluteplayer with deer (hunting-magic context). The second panel portrays the fluteplayer apparently playing tunes for a line of dancers (Fig. 158), while the third shows several fluteplayers with two anthropomorphs and what appears to be a "dancing" deer standing on its hind legs (Fig. 159). Another panel

Figure 157
Petroglyph panel:
fluteplayer with deer,
Indian Creek, Utah.
After Castleton, 1987.

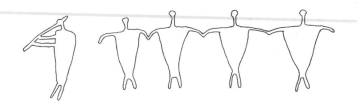

*Figure 158
Petroglyph panel:
fluteplayer with
line of dancers,
Shay Canyon, Utah.*

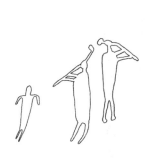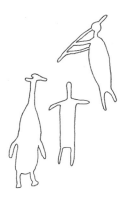

*Figure 159
Petroglyph panel:
fluteplayers with
anthropomorphs and
"dancing" deer,
Shay Canyon, Utah.*

recorded in the Indian Creek drainage depicts two fluteplayers with broad-shouldered anthropomorphs (Fig. A-143). See also Figures A-144, A-145, and A-146.

Near Moab, Utah, fluteplayer images are reported on panels in the Behind the Rocks area and on Mill Creek. On a petroglyph panel in the Behind the Rocks area is a portrayal of a row of humpbacked figures following a humpbacked fluteplayer (Fig. 160), perhaps in ritual procession, in a context of game animals. Another nearby petroglyph panel depicts the fluteplayer in his bird-headed form (see Fig. 116 [page 72]). This type is found at several sites in the Four Corners region and is thought to represent the shaman's magical "soul-flight," as mentioned

Figure 160
Petroglyphs:
humpbacked
fluteplayer
leading line of
"backpacker" figures,
near Moab, Utah.
After Barnes, 1982.

*Figure 161
Petroglyph panel:
humpbacked
fluteplayer with
running figures,
bighorn sheep, and
"fighting"
anthropomorphs,
near Moab, Utah.*

*Figure 162
Petroglyph panel:
humpbacked,
phallic
fluteplayers with
game animal and
paw prints (or
footprints),
Sevenmile Canyon,
Utah.*

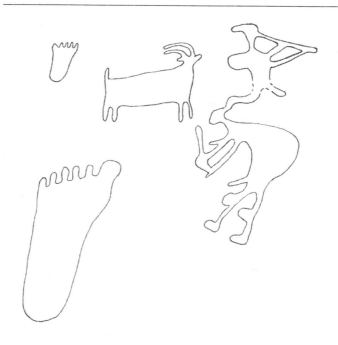

in the description of Canyon de Chelly sites (see page 74). See also Figures 161 and A-147.

To the east of the Green River, in the Island in the Sky District of Canyonlands National Park, there is an early Anasazi petroglyph site on large boulders, on one of which is shown a willowy, phallic fluteplayer bent sharply backwards (Fig. A-148). In nearby Sevenmile Canyon (northwest of Moab) is a petroglyph of two humpbacked fluteplayers, one with knobby knees (Fig. 162). See also Figure 163.

Horseshoe Canyon is located in an isolated part of Canyonlands National Park directly west of the Island in the Sky District of Canyonlands National Park. On a wide, sandstone cliff face at the bottom of the canyon is the type-site for the Barrier Canyon Anthropomorphic Style,[30] dating back at least to the second millennium B.C. Both petroglyphs and pictographs occur in the Barrier Canyon Style, primarily the latter at Utah sites. The usual components of this style are tall, normally armless, broad-shouldered anthropomorphs, often occurring in rows or groups. Facial features are commonly missing; however, prominent, bulging eyes are occasionally depicted. Anthropomorphic figures are frequently associated with zoomorphs, such as snakes, birds, rabbits, and bighorn sheep, as well as with other types of abstract anthropomorphs.

Definite stylistic similarities exist between Barrier Canyon rock art anthropomorphs and unbaked clay figurines from the area. These figurines come from Archaic levels, most of which have been dated to as early as about 4500 B.C.; however, it is not yet possible to securely place the origin of Barrier Canyon Style rock art at such an early date. Mention should be made of the recent C-14 dating of a pigment chip

Figure 163
Petroglyph panel:
large Barrier Canyon
Style anthropomorph
flanked by a series
of humpbacked
figures with staffs,
Sevenmile Canyon,
Utah.

*Figure 164
Pictographs: Barrier
Canyon Style panel
showing a fluteplayer
with an anthropomorph
and a group of tiny
sheep (hunting-magic
context?), south of
Cedar Mountain, Utah.*

*Figure 165
Pictograph panel:
possible fluteplayer
next to an
anthropomorph with
feathered "antenna"
and snakes, south of
Cedar Mountain,
Utah.*

*Figure 166
Petroglyphs:
humpbacked
fluteplayer whose
"flute of light" extends
to head of opposite
figure, Mussentuchit
area, Utah. After sketch
by Jesse Warner.*

from a Barrier Canyon Style pictograph panel in Canyonlands National Park. The chip was taken from a small piece of the panel that had apparently fallen from the rock face. The C-14 date was approximately 3500 B.C.![31] Further research is needed before such early dating of the Barrier Canyon Style will be generally accepted.

Two other Barrier Canyon Style pictograph panels are found on sandstone cliff faces between the San Rafael River and Cedar Mountain (northwest of Green River, Utah). On one panel, a fluteplayer stands next to a similar figure holding a tiny bighorn sheep in the palm of his hand (Fig. 164). The second panel contains a depiction of a tall, bug-eyed fluteplayer (?) next to a larger, shamanlike figure with feathered "antenna" and a snake in each hand (Fig. 165). Should the figures mentioned at the latter two sites indeed be fluteplayers, they would be, by far, the earliest rock art portrayals of this supernatural yet located by the authors. Also, the significance of the fluteplayer in the ideology of that early culture would be accentuated by his being shown as almost equal in size to the only other large anthropomorph on each panel.

Other fluteplayer depictions occur in the Mussentuchit area (Fig. A-149) and Salt Wash (Fig. A-150) of central Utah. At the former site, shadow alignments at certain times of the year create a "flute of light" which gradually extends from the head of the figure on the right to that of the opposite figure (Fig. 166). An odd petroglyph figure that may be a very stylized fluteplayer (Fig. A-151) occurs at a site in the Molen Reef.

Colorado

In Colorado, Anasazi fluteplayer depictions appear to be confined to the southwest quarter. Near the Utah-Colorado border, in La Sal Creek Canyon, an Abajo-La Sal Style[32] panel shows a fluteplayer between two large anthropomorphs (Fig. 167). The Abajo-La Sal Style is typified by broad-shouldered anthropomorphs with triangular or trapezoidal bodies and curved arms held outward. Other elements include quadrupeds, snakes, animal tracks, spirals, lines, and dots.

*Figure 167
Petroglyph panel:
fluteplayers with
anthropomorphs and
unusual spiral,
La Sal Creek, Colorado.
After Cole, 1990.*

On a rock art panel at Mesa Verde is found a "sitting," stick-figure fluteplayer (Fig. A-152); other slender fluteplayer figures are reported on petroglyph panels at Chapin Mesa, Mesa Verde National Park.[33] Nearby Mancos Canyon is the site of a panel depicting a humpbacked, phallic fluteplayer (Fig. A-153). There are reported to be other fluteplayers among the rock art within Ute Mountain Tribal Park, south of Mesa Verde.

In two Hidden Valley rock shelters near Durango, Colorado, Basketmaker II artifacts were

Figure 168
Pictographs: small
fluteplayers, near
Durango, Colorado.
After Daniels, 1954.

found during a site survey in the early 1950s;[34] in one of the shelters there is a rock art panel, apparently Basketmaker III,[35] depicting three very small (about ten centimeters high) pictographs of two black (and one white) nonphallic fluteplayers without humps (Fig. 168).

Fremont Area

The Fremont culture area includes essentially that part of Utah northwest of the Colorado River and overlaps the Anasazi area in some locations; the approximate Fremont date range is A.D. 400 to A.D. 1350 (Figs. 1 and 2). A narrow strip of northwestern Colorado, extending to the Wyoming border area, should also be included as part of the Fremont region. This boundary should be placed somewhat farther to the east, in the upper White River drainage, if two rock art sites in the Beaver Flattop Mountains (east of Meeker, Colorado) are considered to be Fremont rather than Fremont-influenced. These sites, if taken to be Fremont, would push the upper temporal limit of that culture to around A.D. 1500.[36]

The Fremont was a Southwest-related culture that, although practicing horticulture, relied more on wild-food gathering than did the neighboring Anasazi. Fremont settlements were quite small, and kivas did not exist. The Fremont area is divided into five major cultural regions: Sevier, Parowan, Great Salt Lake, San Rafael, and Uinta. Each region is characterized by its own variations in rock art iconography and style.

Along Douglas Creek in the Cañon Pintado National Historic District of west-central Colorado, there is a humpbacked fluteplayer pictograph (Fig. A-154) in red pigment just beneath another pictograph with Barrier Canyon Style figures. This fluteplayer is of indeterminate style and may be transitional between Archaic and Fremont.[37] Other Fremont fluteplayers are reported from the Brown's Park area in northwestern Colorado.[38]

Crossing the border into Utah, we enter the true realm of Fremont culture; most Fremont rock art is to be found in the eastern one-third of the state. This rock art style was strongly influenced by Anasazi motifs from the south[39] (one of which was probably the fluteplayer) and is illustrated on some of the most spectacular and superbly executed panels in the Four Corners states. One of the prime rock art areas in North America is found along Ashley Creek and Dry Fork, west of Vernal. This is one of the type-sites for the Classic Vernal Style, associated with the Uinta Fremont. This unique style is characterized by large, broad-shouldered anthropomorphs with elaborate necklaces, kilts, and head ornaments, all of which likely represent ceremonial regalia, possibly in a shamanic context. This elaboration does not appear to carry over into fluteplayer images, which are quite similar to those found in the Anasazi region. The fluteplayers found on petroglyph panels at these sites are evidently Fremont (Fig. 169 and Figs. A-155, A-156, A-157, and A-158).

A few miles east of Vernal, Utah, along Cub Creek in Dinosaur National Monument, is another Classic Vernal Style rock art area. On a partly eroded petroglyph panel, a humpbacked fluteplayer (Fig. A-159) is depicted near several very large lizard petroglyphs and a few typical Fremont anthropomorphs.

Figure 169
Petroglyph panel:
recumbent fluteplayer
with figures in
ceremonial regalia,
near Vernal, Utah.
After Schaafsma, 1971.

At another site in the monument is an angular
fluteplayer with a pointed hump; this figure is over
three feet tall (Fig. A-160).

Other fluteplayer depictions (probably Fremont)
are reported in Main Canyon, a tributary of Willow
Creek (southeast of Ouray, Utah),[40] in Nine Mile
Canyon, northeast of Price, Utah (Fig. 170), and in

Figure 170
Petroglyph panel:
fluteplayers with
sheep and snake,
Nine Mile Canyon,
Utah.
After photo by
Margie Crouse.

Figure 171
Petroglyph:
humpbacked
fluteplayer,
Capitol Reef National
Park, Utah.

Capitol Reef National Park, where a fluteplayer is
shown "emerging" from a shaman's horn (see Fig.
122 [page 75]). Also in the park are petroglyphs of an
expressive, humpbacked fluteplayer (Fig. 171) and
two "backpacker" figures holding planting sticks or
canes (Fig. A-161).

Mogollon Area

The Mogollon culture region covers approximately the southern half of New Mexico as far east as the Pecos River, the northern parts of Chihuahua and Sonora, Mexico, and southeastern Arizona about as far north as the Little Colorado River (Fig. 1).

This mountain-and-desert culture involved a complex series of developments and a period of major changes with far-reaching consequences for the history of the Southwest. Horticultural activities began very early in the Mogollon region, but village living did not actually commence until around 300 B.C. Incipient Mogollon culture is considered to have emerged from the Archaic around 100 B.C. These villages consisted of relatively small groupings of pit houses until about A.D. 1000, after which time aboveground, pueblo-type structures became prevalent.

The rock art of the western Mogollon is divided into the Mogollon Red Style and its subcategory, the Reserve Petroglyph Style, whereas that of the eastern Mogollon is composed of an early Abstract Style (prior to A.D. 1000) and the Jornada Style. The latter includes the rock art of both the Jornada and Mimbres regions. By around A.D. 1400, the creation of rock art ceased in most of the Mogollon region.[41]

Compared to the Anasazi and Fremont culture areas, there are few fluteplayer depictions in the rock art of the Mogollon region. There was a possible fluteplayer portrayal near Reserve, New Mexico,[42] but the site has been destroyed by road building. Within the Mimbres area, there is a petroglyph of a humpbacked anthropomorph holding a crook at a site near Cooke's Peak, New Mexico (Fig. 172).

*Figure 172
Petroglyph:
humpbacked
anthropomorph
holding crook, near
Cooke's Peak,
New Mexico.*

In the Jornada Style area east of the Rio Grande, a humpbacked, phallic, ogrelike figure at the extensive Three Rivers, New Mexico, petroglyph site may represent Kokopelli, although lacking a flute (see Fig. 189). In comparing this figure with one in an Awatovi kiva mural painting in the Hopi area (see Fig. 188 and Section IV, page 117), the natural rock protrusion in the waist area may be analogous to the ear of corn stuck in the "belt" of the Awatovi figure (said to possibly represent Kokopelli).[43] Also at Three Rivers is a petroglyph that appears to represent a phallic fluteplayer (Fig. 173) and another depicting two humpbacked, phallic figures holding a corn plant (Fig. A-162).

There are no other known fluteplayer rock art portrayals farther south in the Mogollon culture region; however, there is a humpbacked, phallic figure (Fig. 174) on a petroglyph panel north of Fort Hancock, Texas. This figure is located in a small enclosure formed by the vertical faces of three large boulders and may have been a fertility shrine. There is also a humpbacked, phallic figure with a female portrayed on a pictograph panel (see Fig. 31, page 33) in Comanche Cave at Hueco Tanks State Park, east of El Paso, Texas. This figure, thought to be of Apache origin, is fluteless, and no other Kokopelli types are recorded in this region.

Hohokam Area

It is believed that the Hohokam had Mesoamerican origins, arriving in the area around A.D. 300 from the south. Anthropologist Emil W. Haury[44] assigned a much earlier date (300 B.C.) based on his work at the Snaketown site; this has been revised by subsequent research to a considerably later time frame. At the time of their migration to this region, they already lived in villages and had developed pottery making and an extensive irrigation system. The Hohokam evidently imported the use of ball courts and temple mounds from the south. Their villages consisted of small groupings of houses until the Classic Period (A.D. 1150 to A.D. 1450), at which time sizeable adobe complexes and large houses began to predominate.

Figure 173
Petroglyph:
phallic
fluteplayer (?),
Three Rivers,
New Mexico.

Figure 174
Petroglyph:
humpbacked, phallic
figure, near
Fort Hancock, Texas.

Figure 176
Petroglyphs
(Hohokam): pair of
fluteplayers,
Sierra Estrella,
Arizona. After photo by
Janet Golio.

Figure 177
Petroglyph
(Hohokam):
humpbacked
fluteplayer with game
animal on flute, Aztec
Canyon, Arizona.
After Steward, 1929.

The Hohokam apparently spoke a Piman variant of the Uto-Aztecan language group that could be comprehended by people living as far north as the Salt River in Arizona and southward to what is today the state of Jalisco in Mexico. The Pima and Tohono O'Odham (formerly Papago) are probably descendants of the Hohokam.

Fluteplayer images within the Hohokam culture area of southern Arizona appear to be almost totally confined to pottery representations, which are addressed in Section IV. The paucity of fluteplayer representations in Hohokam rock art can apparently be explained merely as a regional cultural variation with its roots in previous Archaic patterns. In fact, anthropomorphic forms of any type are relatively infrequent in Hohokam rock art when compared to the Anasazi and Fremont areas, and are usually of the stick-figure or simple full-figure variety. One fluteplayer petroglyph has been reported from a South Mountain site near Phoenix (Fig. 175), and two others are recorded from a site in the Sierra Estrella (Fig. 176), on the southwest outskirts of Phoenix. An unusual stick-figure, humpbacked fluteplayer with a game animal (?) standing on his flute (hunting-magic context) was depicted at a canyon site several miles south of Phoenix (Fig. 177).

They had become a procession led by Kokopelli who strode across the mesa, playing his flute, calling now and then in reply to greetings, his confident step setting his luxurious mantle swinging. His shining ear ornaments swayed gracefully and the turquoise beads on his cap were in constant motion. The bright feathers on his cap stirred in the wind as if they were alive. The brilliant macaw riding his shoulder was the final dramatic touch.

. . . From cave to cave shouts relayed the news of Kokopelli's arrival. Runners sped through the canyon with details. The music of the flute, the barking of dogs, the whoop of children, and a babble of voices flooded the canyon with excitement. "Kokopelli comes! There will be feasting! There will be ceremonies! There will be stories and singing and dancing! Kokopelli comes!"

. . . "Kokopelli comes! He of the singing reed, he of the sacred seed, comes to assure the fertility and good fortune of our people. . . ."

Every woman, every girl, fingered the secret amulet known only to her . . . "Make him choose me!" each one prayed. . . .

—Linda Lay Shuler,
She Who Remembers

Fluteplayer Images in Ceramics and Kiva Murals

N umerous portrayals of the fluteplayer in ceramics and, to a lesser extent, in kiva murals, attest to the importance of this supernatural being in the prehistoric pantheon. It is interesting and pertinent to compare depictions of the fluteplayer in other media with those in rock art. Again, most of these portrayals occur in the Anasazi culture region, primarily in the middle and later Pueblo phases.

Ceramics

Figure 178
Pueblo I black-on-white bowl, fluteplayer with humpbacked archer, Mesa Verde, Colorado. Photo by Kelly. Courtesy of National Park Service.

A substantial number of fluteplayer depictions on pottery are found in the literature. A Pueblo I black-on-white bowl (Fig. 178) from Mesa Verde shows the fluteplayer with a humpbacked archer; the interior portion below the rim is composed of rows of ducks (hunting deity context). On another black-on-white Mesa Verde bowl (Pueblo II/III), a phallic, humpbacked Kokopelli is depicted as an isolated figure surrounded by a stepped design (Fig. 179). In the bottom of a Mancos Black-on-white bowl (ca. A.D. 1100-1150), a cross-legged Kokopelli is portrayed on one side of a horned lizard, a mountain sheep on the other

(Fig. 180). Other ceramic designs from Mesa Verde depicting fluteplayers are shown in Figures A-163 and A-164. A black-on-white Anasazi bowl (Fig. 181) from the Dolores River drainage in extreme southwestern Colorado depicts Kokopelli with a female figure (fertility context).

Figure 179
Kokopelli fugure from black-on-white Mesa Verde bowl, southwestern Colorado. After photo courtesy of National Park Service.

The interior design of a Sikyatki Polychrome bowl (Pueblo IV) from Awatovi (Hopi) portrays a phallic, seated figure carrying a small rider piggyback (possibly analogous to hump?) and holding an indeterminate

Figure 180
Mancos Black-on-
white bowl, Kokopelli
with horned lizard and
bighorn sheep,
southwestern
Colorado.
Donated to the
Permanent Collections
of the Museum of New
Mexico in 1993 by
Joseph L. Cramer of
Denver.

Figure 181
Black-on-white
Anasazi bowl,
Kokopelli with female,
Dolores River drainage,
Colorado.
Courtesy of BLM,
Anasazi Heritage
Center,
Dolores, Colorado.

object (feathered prayer stick, planting cane, dance wand?). The opposite side of the bowl's interior contains a female figure (Fig. 182) with arms and legs spread, possibly representing Kokopelmana (see Section V).[1]

*Figure 182 (above, left)
Interior design of
Sikyatki Polychrome
bowl with phallic,
seated figure and
female. Reprinted
courtesy of the Peabody
Museum of
Archaeology and
Ethnology, Harvard
University.*

*Figure 183 (above, right)
Black-on-white Anasazi
bowl with insectiform,
humpbacked fluteplayer,
Zuni Reservation,
New Mexico.
From Roberts, 1932.*

From the Village of the Great Kivas, a Chacoan outlier east of Zuni, comes a black-on-white bowl (Pueblo II to III) with a fret design around the interior rim. The single figure in the bottom is an insectiform, humpbacked fluteplayer (Fig. 183).

An unusual Gallup Black-on-white effigy pitcher comes from a stone masonry site in northwestern New Mexico (Fig. 184). Many effigy vessels of this type are bird-shaped; however, this Pueblo III pitcher appears to represent Kokopelli with separately molded arms ending in hands holding a flute, the latter actually forming the handle. The curve of the bottom and back of the pitcher would seem to form the hump. On the upper surface of the vessel on either side of the neck are painted two figures, one a phallic male (Kokopelli?), the other a female (Kokopelmana?).[2] Such an unusual pitcher may have been used in a fertility ritual rather than for mundane domestic purposes.

A number of Anasazi fluteplayer depictions are found on pottery sherds, such as the humpbacked figure (Fig. A-185) shown on a sherd from a small Santa

*Figure 184
Gallup Black-on-white
effigy pitcher in shape of
fluteplayer,
northwestern
New Mexico.*

Fe Black-on-white bowl found at Paa-ko, a Pueblo IV ruin east of the Sandia Mountains, New Mexico.[3] Other fluteplayer depictions are found on several additional Anasazi (and on many Hohokam) pottery sherds.

The Hohokam usually portrayed the fluteplayer alone or in decorative rows of identical figures, with three to eight backward-directed head appendages, presumably feathers.[4] The Hohokam fluteplayer normally has an arched body without a definite hump and is apparently never portrayed in the phallic mode. A collection of twenty-eight sherds of Hohokam pottery from Snaketown shows the fluteplayer figure; only once do the body configuration and the two forward antennas suggest the features of an insect.[5] The Gila Butte phase (about

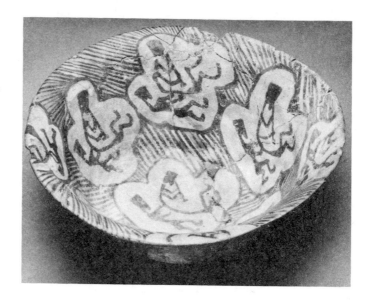

A.D. 750 to A.D. 850) is evidently the earliest in which the fluteplayer appears on Hohokam pottery. The interior of a small Hohokam bowl (Fig. 185) contains several randomly placed, lobed areas in each of which an arched fluteplayer is depicted with a "dancing" figure holding on to his back. The dancing figures are much more realistically portrayed than the fluteplayers, which are essentially of the stick-figure type, although quite animated. This bowl is unusual in the random layout of its decoration; most Hohokam bowls have interior designs divided into nearly identical quadrants or other forms of equal sectoring. Some type of symmetry is usually present. Considering the numerous fluteplayer depictions on Hohokam pottery, it is amazing that rock art portrayals of this important supernatural are almost nonexistent in that culture (see Section III, page 106).

Although fluteplayer images are also rare in the rock art of the Mimbres region, several possible

Kokopelli-type depictions were found on Mimbres bowls; these figures are humpbacked and phallic, and one holds a crook (see Fig. A-4).

Kiva Murals

"The Pueblo Indians of the American Southwest first began to paint murals on the walls of their structures about A.D. 1000 [Pueblo II]," writes Constance S. Silver. "This tradition has continued to the present, and, today, the United States possesses an important corpus of mural art of considerable antiquity and artistic value."[6]

The most impressive of these murals are painted on kiva walls, many of which have numerous layers of plaster containing successive paintings done over long periods of time; one kiva wall at Awatovi boasted more than one hundred layers of plaster![7]

One of the best-preserved and earliest kiva murals yet discovered (ca. A.D. 1200) was found at a site near Chaco Canyon in northwestern New Mexico.[8] The main figures on the kiva bench are three fluteplayers painted in red on a white background (Fig. 186). The fluteplayer was obviously important here, since there are no other figures on the bench face—only a few incised handprints (perhaps the

*Figure 186
Kiva mural:
humpbacked
fluteplayers painted on
kiva bench, near Chaco
Canyon, New Mexico.
After Brody, 1991.*

painter's signature) and several depictions of moun-
tainlike elements.

An incised plaster wall in an eleventh-century
kiva at Chaco Canyon, New Mexico, contains a hunting scene (hunting-magic context) which includes a
humpbacked fluteplayer and archers (Fig. 187). This
mural scene was executed on the fifth plaster layer of
a thirty-one layer total.[9]

Figure 187
Kiva mural painting:
hunting scene with
fluteplayer and archers,
Chaco Canyon,
New Mexico.
After Brody, 1991.

An elaborate wall painting was found during
the excavation of Awatovi, a Hopi village destroyed
by neighboring conservative factions during the
winter of A.D. 1700-1701, reputedly for having
accepted Spanish missionaries after the 1680 Pueblo
Revolt. On one wall a humpbacked, phallic figure is
depicted in profile (Fig. 188), painted blue with a
white phallus having a red tip. He has an ear of corn
stuck in his narrow red belt, perhaps to offer as a
gift (or bribe) to the female, portrayed in frontal
view, next to him. She is painted yellow with a
white vulva and black hands. Above the figures is
an upside-down creature with a body painted blue
and a black face or mask with white features; this
may represent Kokopelmana, who has a similar
mask.[10] The Kokopelli-like figure may be analogous to a similar petroglyph depiction (Fig. 189) at
Three Rivers, New Mexico, described in Section III

Figure 188
Kiva mural painting:
humpbacked, phallic
figure with female and
possible Kokopelmana
depiction, Awatovi
(Antelope Mesa),
Arizona.
Courtesy of Peabody
Museum, Harvard
University.
Photo by Fogg
Museum, 1942.

as having a protrusion at his waist, perhaps also representing an ear of corn.

In the mid-nineteenth century, a kiva mural painting recorded at Jemez Pueblo, New Mexico, depicted two figures playing their flutes over baskets of corn sitting on what appear to be cloud terraces, a rainbow arching across the scene (rain-bringing and fertility context). The fluteplayers are painted in white, and wear long, knee-length garments and wide-brimmed hats (Fig. 190).

Phallic, mountain-goat archers with humped backs were portrayed on a kiva mural at Fire Temple, Mesa Verde, previously described in Section II (see Fig. 13 [page 22]). These figures do not carry flutes but may relate to Kokopelli in his hunting-magic context.

Figure 189
Petroglyph panel:
phallic, humpbacked
figure, Three Rivers,
New Mexico.

Figure 190
Kiva mural painting:
figures playing flutes
over baskets of corn,
Jemez Pueblo,
New Mexico.
After Brody, 1991.

Two other Kokopelli/kiva connections are quite unusual. In 1980, excavations at Yellow Jacket Canyon in southwestern Colorado revealed a Pueblo III Period kiva which had an interesting floor feature. Encircling half of the kiva, a large, phallic figure of Kokopelli had been carved into the floor, filled with clay, and plastered over.[11] At Sand Canyon, another Pueblo III site about six miles southwest of the Yellow Jacket site, a second kiva with an unusual subfloor feature was excavated. A stylized, phallic Kokopelli figure had been pecked and incised into a smoothed portion of the bedrock surface after which the entire kiva floor was covered with compacted fill (Fig. 191).[12] These two subfloor Kokopelli figures, being hidden from view, evidently had an esoteric, magico-religious purpose intended to enhance the horticultural and human fertility of the pueblo. Perhaps this was especially important at a time when prolonged drought caused fertility rates to diminish.

After examining the myriad guises of Kokopelli as well as the immense spread over time and space of fluteplayer images in various media, and rock art in particular, we cannot doubt the importance that this mythical being held in the lives of the prehistoric peoples of the Southwest.

Figure 191
Kiva petroglyph:
stylized, phallic
fluteplayer, Sand
Canyon, Colorado.
After Bradley, 1989.

*A man traveled through this country with a bag
of corn seed over one shoulder. His shadow against the
desert looked like a deformity. He would stop at every
village and teach the people how to plant corn. And then
when the sun slipped behind the mesa and the village was
asleep, he would walk through the corn fields playing his
flute. The seeds would flower, pushing themselves up
through the red, sandy soil and follow the high-pitched
notes upward. The sun would rise and the man would be
gone, with corn stalks the height of a young girl
shimmering in the morning light. Many of the young
women would complain of a fullness in their bellies. The
elders would smile, knowing they were pregnant. They
would look to the southwest and call him "Kokopelli."*

— Terry Tempest Williams,
"Kokopelli's Return"

Myths and Stories

The American Southwest, where ethnological analogs often complement archaeological research (especially in the Anasazi region), provides opportunities to interpret the past through the myths, rituals, and stories of contemporary native peoples. The Hopi are the source of the Kokopelli kachina and most of our information about him. Likewise, there are counterparts for Kokopelli from other pueblos, notably Acoma and Zuni.

Kokopelli as a Hopi Kachina

Kachinas are benevolent supernaturals, revered ancestor spirits, associated with clouds and rain. They bring rain and well-being to the people, and are personified in the masked dancers at the pueblos.[1] Rock art studies indicate the kachina cult arrived in the Pueblo area in the fourteenth century from the Jornada Mogollon region to the south,[2] although it is not clear whether the cult was adopted directly or whether the Pueblo people created it by selectively embracing certain preexisting Mogollon themes. The rock art style changed significantly about A.D. 1325 in the Puebloan world—along the northern Rio Grande Valley and its tributaries, as well as at Zuni and Hopi. In this new Rio Grande Style rock art, there is a proliferation of mask representations and kachina-like figures.

As a Hopi kachina, Kokopelli varies somewhat in appearance between villages, and, like many kachinas, has a variety of forms in which he can appear (see Figure 192 for one version of the Hopi Kokopelli kachina). On Second Mesa, the Kokopelli mask has a straight snout made of corn husks, whereas on Third Mesa his corn-husk snout points upward and he wears a white shirt with orange stitching. He is always concerned with increase and fertility among the people, animals, and plants. His rain making ensures good crops of corn and other food. When he appears in dances, usually in the spring, he is erotic. He wears a black mask with a white stripe and has a long snout.[3] At dances in the past, he displayed his genitals, but this has evolved into a costume involving an exaggerated false penis constructed from a gourd. He carries no flute, but it is believed that his long snout represents a nose whistle. He has a humped back or wears a bag on his back, and may carry a stick and rattle. His habit of chasing females, simulating copulation, and "humping" spectators was frowned upon as obscene by early anthropologists, tourists, and priests, but the Hopi do not look upon his behavior as lewd,[4] since sexual manifestations are

*Figure 192
Kokopelli
Kachina Doll,
Hopi, ca. 1920-1930.
Blair Clark,
photographer,
School of American
Research Collections in
the Museum of New
Mexico, 1243/12.*

not considered taboo but merely a fact of life. Kokopelli used to figure more prominently in Hopi dances but is seen infrequently now, apparently having been suppressed for his ribald routine.

We have this description of a Kokopelli kachina dance in a kiva at Hopi in 1934:[5]

There were six Kokopele dancers. They wore dark gray masks, and suits of long underwear with a woman's belt tied at the back. Every performer had a hump fixed on his shoulders, and a large red "penis" (of gourd?) strapped in position over the underwear. Each dancer carried a rattle in one hand and held his "penis" with the other throughout the performance. As they entered the kiva the katchinas lunged at the spectators, particularly at the women. They sang and danced facing the audience, advancing in unison occasionally and singing a slow song. The spectators laughed hilariously. Afterwards a Hopi man told Dr. Eggan one should be friends with the Kokopele as they were the ones who sent babies.

Kokopelli's Female Counterpart

Hopi kachinas are sometimes represented in both male and female forms. The female counterpart to Kokopelli is called Kokopelmana.[6] This is a "racing" kachina, and the role is played by strong runners who chase male spectators and simulate copulation with those who are caught. From the same source as the dance description given above is this 1934 description of Kokopelmana at a Hopi ceremonial:

> Kokopelmana . . . appeared barefooted and barelegged, wearing a ragged manta, a shabby ata'u (small ceremonial blanket worn by women), and a mask comparable to that of Kokopeltiyo. As soon as this impersonator emerged from the kiva, all the men and boys in the vicinity began to scatter. At first the Kokopelmana merely feinted running after them, but suddenly "she"

caught up with an unwary man, raised him high in "her" arms and pretended to copulate with him from behind. This done, "she" released him and handed him a few packets of somiviki (corn-meal cakes). From then on "she" ran far and wide in quest of "lovers," pretended to lure men out of their houses, and argued in vigorous pantomime with all women and girls who tried to keep men away from "her" . . . the Oraibi people said that a man was "spoiled" (that is, rendered undesirable to other girls) if the Kokopelmana "got into him."

Kokopelli Goes Courting

An interesting story of Kokopelli derives from the Hopi mesas, as follows:[7]

At the time when Oraibi was first inhabited, the katcina Kokopele was living nearby with his grandmother. Within the village there dwelt a good-looking girl who was so vain (qwivi) that she rejected the advances of all the young men. . . . Kokopele confided to his grandmother that he meant to try his luck with this pretty girl, but his grandmother laughed at him because he was humpbacked and far homelier than many of the Oraibi boys. . . . Kokopele had noticed that. . . . the girl was in the habit of going to a particular spot at the edge of the mesa to perform her natural functions. . . . His first step was to dig a trench leading from his house to the exact spot which the girl was accustomed to visit. Then he

cut and hollowed out a number of reeds, fashioned them into a continuous pipe, and laid it in
the ditch . . . he filled in the trench and smoothed
it over . . . the next day the girl came to the spot.
. . . Hardly had she finished than she felt something stirring under her, and enjoying the sensation, made no effort to investigate. It was the
penis of Kokopele that she felt, for so cleverly
had he arranged his hollow tube that on insert-
ing his organ into it at home he was enabled,
thanks to its unusual length, to direct it into the
girl's vagina. From then on Kokopele never
failed to take advantage of his device nor did the
girl abandon her customary visits to this spot. At
last she found herself pregnant, but neither she
nor any of the people in the village had the
slightest idea of her lover's identity . . . when in
due time a boy was born to her, his paternity
was as much a mystery as ever.

The question of the child's paternity was resolved
that spring when the village held a footrace for all the
men and boys. They picked bouquets of flowers, ran
with them, and presented them to the baby as they
finished the race. The baby would accept flowers
only from the runner who was his father. The baby
would not take the flowers from any of the runners
until Kokopelli, who finished the race last, offered his
bouquet. When the child accepted Kokopelli's flowers, the village knew he was the father. The villagers
told the girl to take the kachina home and keep him
for her husband. This she was happy to do, for as a
kachina, Kokopelli was a good provider and brought
lots of rain.

This myth is apparently depicted in a petroglyph from the Jemez Mountains of New Mexico, shown in Figure 193 (see also page 55). A similar version of this Kokopelli story is recorded from Acoma Pueblo:[8]

A long time ago two Dapopo brothers lived at Acoma near the house of Masewi, the elder of the twin war gods. The younger Dapopo asked the War Chief's daughter to let him sleep with her but she refused. Then the older Dapopo asked her the same thing but was also refused. In fact, the chief's daughter rejected the advances of all the boys at Acoma. The Dapopos were angry and kept thinking of how they could get the girl. At last the older brother advised the younger to dig a hole in the ground at the side of the mesa and hide there until the girl came to relieve herself in the evening. In this way the Dapopo got his girl. She did not realize exactly what had happened, but she liked the sensation so much that she repeatedly returned to the same spot. Then the older brother hid and he too got the girl.

Soon the Acoma people noticed that she was going to have a baby. . . . When the time came two babies were born, one for each of the Dapopo. The War Chief decided to find out who had fathered his daughter's children so he announced a test. All the young men and boys of the village went out and gathered bunches of flowers. Then they lined up and offered them to the babies but they would not accept them. Finally the Dapopos, who were last in line, presented their flowers and the children took them, thus acknowledging the Dapopos for their fathers.

Figure 193
Petroglyph panel:
Kokopelli in coitus
with female
(dotted line represents
juncture of two vertical
rock faces),
Holiday Mesa,
New Mexico.

Kokopelli as a Zuni Kachina

Figure 194
Petroglyphs:
possible depiction of the
kachina Ololowishkya
and female figure
with metate,
Zuni Reservation,
New Mexico.

There are certain Zuni kachinas that share similarities with the Hopi's Kokopelli kachina and with the humpbacked fluteplayers depicted in rock art of the Zuni area.[9] Paiyatamu is a fluteplaying culture hero, but he is not humpbacked. Like Kokopelli, however, he is associated with fertility and rain. The kachina Owiwi is described by the Zunis as humpbacked or carrying a pack of fetishes on his back. There is also at Zuni a phallic kachina who has no hump, known as Ololowishkya (Fig. 194). He is the central figure in a ceremony with flute playing and grinding of corn by men dressed as women. This ceremony has been described by contemporary Zunis:[10]

It's embarrassing, but it was for religious doings. Some males dressed like females and stretched out with grinding stones. There were fluteplayers and rain dancers. Ololowishkya had a dingaling made out of a gourd. He peed a sweet syrup into a big pot that had sweet corn in it. He peed to the directions of the earth six times. He made balls of the juice and corn and gave it to everyone. It tasted good. This ceremony was done so there wouldn't be any problem with men's urine. We don't do this now because white people watch.

Another connection between Zuni and Hopi is implied in the form that Kokopelli takes at the Hopi village of Hano. Here he appears as a big black man, known as Nepokwa'i, who carries a buckskin bag on his back. Even the kachina dolls of this figure are painted black. Nepokwa'i may be based on the Moorish slave Esteban, who accompanied Marcos de Niza's 1539 expedition; Esteban was stoned to death at Zuni for molesting their women. The Tewa people of Hano had lived with the Zunis prior to settling in the Hopi region.[11]

From the rich oral tradition at Zuni, some narrative poems have been recorded and translated.[12] One performance, lasting forty minutes, relates a story about the flute-playing Nepayatamu (Paiyatamu) and his medicine-society kin. He is brought back to life by singing and drumming after being wrongly killed, and then leads his brothers in revenge on his wrongdoers. When he blows on his flute, a big swallowtail butterfly comes out of it, and when he sucks on his flute the swallowtail goes back into it.

Nepayatamu sends the butterfly to his enemies, who are certain women, one of whom was responsible for his death. The swallowtail sprinkles the women with his wing powder when they try to catch him in order to use his pattern in their basketry. This makes the women go crazy, and he leads them to

Nepayatamu, who is perched up in a cottonwood tree. The women try to catch the butterfly by throwing their clothes at him, until eventually they are naked. When they lie down to rest in the shadow of the cottonwood tree, Nepayatamu spits on them and they go to sleep.

Nepayatamu then summons his grandfathers (ancestors), who come out of hiding and have pleasure with the sleeping women. When the women awake, they find Nepayatamu still sitting in the tree with his legs dangling down. He sucks the swallowtail back into his flute. He throws down leaves, and these become blankets in which the women dress themselves. Then Nepayatamu leads the women to his house, where they are fed; and then he leads them towards the place where the sun comes out. Only they get tired and keep falling down. When Nepayatamu sucks on his flute the elder sister, the killer, goes inside it. Then he blows, and a flock of white moths come out. The woman becomes moths, and he tells her, "Now, this is the life you will live, so that when spring is near you will be a sign of its coming."[13] Eventually, he turns all the other women into moths, too.

Nepayatamu goes on to meet his father, the sun, who praises his way of getting revenge on the women. In this way, the Clown Society was created long ago.

The Water Jar Boy

Fluteplayers within several petroglyph panels (Fig. 195) at La Cienega, New Mexico, are integral components as metaphors that may illustrate the Tewa myth of the Water Jar Boy.[14] This myth from Pueblo oral

tradition contains some common elements and recurring themes, such as a girl who does not want to marry; a supernatural conception; and the son of the virgin birth asking, "Who is my father?" and then setting forth to seek his father. In this particular myth, the girl becomes pregnant when mud gets into her while she is mixing it for her mother's pottery. She gives birth to a little water jar that grows into a boy within the jar. Later the boy cracks the confining pot on a rock while rolling down a hill during a rabbit hunt with his grandfather. After emerging from the pot, he goes on a quest for his father, whom he eventually finds living inside a spring. The boy and his mother later go to live with his father there.

The proposal that these particular panels at La Cienega metaphorically illustrate the elements and sequence of events of the Water Jar Boy myth is interesting. For instance, a row of phallic fluteplayers is explained as young Pueblo men going "wife hunting," carrying gifts for brides in their packs and playing flutes to court them. These suitors are all going in the same direction (none returning, to suggest having been chosen), which may indicate that none of them was responsible for the birth which is depicted

Figure 195
Petroglyph panel:
possible portrayal of
Water Jar Boy myth,
La Cienega,
New Mexico.
After Patterson-
Rudolph, 1990.

nearby. Other aspects of the myth are said to be portrayed in animal or bird form in the petroglyph panel
to symbolize the attributes of people portrayed in the
myth. The power of metaphor is used in both myth
and petroglyphs to present fundamental themes in
the Pueblo universe.

Kokopelli as an Insect

The transfiguration of Kokopelli into an insectlike
being has been discussed. The locust is one of the
most revered insects, and is featured in the Hopi
emergence myth. Kokopelli has been identified with
the character of locust, who is patron of the Hopi
flute societies. In the emergence myth, Locust was
sent up from the lower world to seek an exit for man.
When the clouds shot their bolts through him, he
went on playing his flute.[15] The flute societies have
locust medicine to dream the future, and pieces of
locusts are thrown on the fire to hasten the return of
warm weather. Locust plays the flute to melt the
snow when appealed to by the sun-loving snakes.[16]
This may help explain the common association of
humpbacked fluteplayers with snakes in rock art
(Fig. 196).

Kokopelli as Trickster

In all his many guises, Kokopelli has been proposed as
a southwest manifestation of the universal Trickster
archetype.[17] In this role, he shares traits with many
characters from other Native American regions:

Wakdjunkaga and Hare (the buffoon and culture hero of the Winnebago tribe), Wisaka of the Fox Indians, Sitconski of the Assiniboine, Ishtinike of the Ponca, Nixant of the Gros Ventre, Iktomi (Spider) of the Oglala-Sioux, Nanabozho or Glooscap of the Algonkians, and Raven of the Northwest Coast tribes.[18] Tricksters are transformers and appear in animal disguise (Raven, Coyote, Hare, Spider). Similarly, the humpbacked fluteplayer has been depicted in rock art of the Southwest in the form of various creatures.

    A comparison of Kokopelli with the Winnebago Trickster Wakdjunkaga illustrates many parallels.[19] Both are notorious for their sexuality, as symbolized in each by a large phallus. Wakdjunkaga seduces the chief's daughter, and Kokopelli cleverly impregnates the most sought-after girl in the village. Wakdjunkaga carries his penis coiled up in a box on his back, whereas Kokopelli (and Ghanaskidi) carries seeds in

Figure 196
Petroglyph panel:
phallic, humpbacked
fluteplayer with snake,
La Cieneguilla,
New Mexico.

his hump. In some accounts both characters are said to carry songs in their backpacks. Wakdjunkaga can change into a woman; the Kokopelli kachina has the female Kokopelmana counterpart.

Scholars, including Carl Jung, have compared the North American Indian Trickster to manifestations elsewhere in the world. The humpbacked fluteplayer of the Southwest is perhaps a mythological cousin of other fertility figures such as Pan and Orpheus, also musicians. Such archetypes survive from the early stages of human consciousness and may predate the shaman.[20] One scholar states that Kokopelli "may be compared with the universal Trickster archetype, who, in spite of his unrestrained sexuality, in his roles as hunting magician and rain priest changes from an unprincipled amoral force into a creator who brings order and security into the chaos of the world."[21]

Kokopelli is everywhere, along with whole tribes of fellow rock-art figures in what is nothing less than a tidal change in the sociocultural currents of Western art. Coyotes are out, Kokopellis are in . . .

And this spooky, jaunty fellow with the humpback, the flute, and the erect phallus, what of him? Why do all these people want to take him and his beguiling cousins home with them? Well, maybe he is magic, maybe he and the other powerful symbols we call petroglyphs do contain some mystical ancient force. Maybe the hands of the artists who carved him and his fellow rock figures were moved by some elemental command that stirs us, too. Touching something deep inside themselves, they thus managed to pull off the old abracadabra that is every artist's dream: to reach across time to touch us, too, with their bold, stark, mysterious talismans, poetry in stone that speaks in a language we didn't even know we understood.

— John Neary,
"Kokopelli Kitsch"

Conclusion

Due to a greater appreciation of our prehistoric heritage, and perhaps because of his universally appealing archetypal nature, Kokopelli (and rock art in general) is currently more popular than ever. Contemporary images of the fluteplayer are becoming a common sight in the arts, crafts, and commerce of the Southwest. To list a few, there are Kokopelli-inspired motels and stores, galleries, nightclubs, realty offices, rafting companies, jewelry, T-shirts, and recorder societies. There is even a Kokopelli Trail for mountain bikes on public lands in Colorado and Utah. In the tourist mecca of Santa Fe, the once ubiquitous "howling coyote" image is apparently being replaced with Kokopelli, another Trickster.

Interestingly, the great majority of these contemporary applications use the .fluteplayer image from Hohokam ceramics (Fig. 25) for Kokopelli, a misleading irony since the Hohokam character lacks hump and phallus and is only marginally related to Kokopelli the kachina and the classic Anasazi/Pueblo humpbacked fluteplayer. This form of "Kokopelli" has become a popular regional icon that, although lacking the full richness of the classic humpbacked fluteplayer, nevertheless transcends temporal and cultural barriers and is a source of fascination for many.

No matter what his form or how complete our understanding of his history, Kokopelli still brings wonder to our lives. The thin sound of his flute that once echoed off canyon walls must still be reverberating around the Southwest and through the ages. We will be hearing more about him in the years to come as his popularity grows.

    . . . Walk toward the sun. After a time you will come to the barrier at the edge of the world. Descend into a canyon. If your heart is good and your spirit young, Raven will show you the way. Make no loud plans, for Coyote will be nearby. . . . Massive walls, old before time, offer shade. A scent of water listens. And something else. Barely hidden, a river of time runs deep here, unbridged by man. It carries you to the paintings.

    . . . The people never left the canyon. As the paintings gained depth and life, the people faded, became translucent, were swallowed as sound is swallowed here, returned to the rock.

    This I saw at the place of paintings. Kokopelli still wanders these canyons. The sly old rock musician may be disguised as a tourist, but certain characteristics are diagnostic. The small daypack. The tendency to lick his lips as he studies the women. Do not trade with this man. Maintain a respectful silence, a discrete distance. He will not stay long. . . .

As I lingered there I felt the pull of the rock. The air seemed thicker somehow. Before I could see the solid walls through the flesh of my body, I came away.

— Clay Johnson,
   "Clay's Tablet (Barrier Canyon)"

Notes

Section I: INTRODUCTION

1. Polly Schaafsma, *Indian Rock Art of the Southwest* (Santa Fe and Albuquerque, N.M.: School of American Research and University of New Mexico Press, 1980), 136; Etienne B. Renaud, "Kokopelli: A Study in Pueblo Mythology," *Southwestern Lore* 14, no.2 (1948): 25.
2. Polly Schaafsma, *Indian Rock Art of the Southwest*, 136.
3. Campbell Grant, *Rock Art of the American Indian* (third printing; Dillon, Colo.: Vistabooks, 1992), 60; Campbell Grant, *Canyon de Chelly: Its People and Rock Art* (Tucson: University of Arizona Press, 1978), 213.
4. Klaus F. Wellmann, "Kokopelli of Indian Paleology: Hunchbacked Rain Priest, Hunting Magician, and Don Juan of the Old Southwest," *Journal of the American Medical Association* 212 (1970): 1682; Hugh C. Cutler, "Medicine Men and the Preservation of a Relict Gene in Maize," *Journal of Heredity* 35 (1944): 291-94.

5. Campbell Grant, *Rock Art of the American Indian,* 60; Frank Waters, "Kokopilau: The Humpbacked Flute Player," *Shaman's Drum* 10 (Fall 1987): 19.

6. Klaus F. Wellmann, "Kokopelli of Indian Paleology," 1682.

7. Hugh C. Cutler, "Medicine Men and the Preservation of a Relict Gene in Maize," 291-94.

8. Florence Hawley, "Kokopelli of the Prehistoric Southwestern Pueblo Pantheon," *American Anthropologist* 39 (1937): 644-46.

9. Polly Schaafsma, "Kachinas in Rock Art," *Journal of New World Archaeology* 4, no. 2 (1981): 30.

Section II: THE MANY GUISES AND RELATIONS OF THE HUMPBACKED FLUTEPLAYER

1. Campbell Grant, *Canyon de Chelly: Its People and Rock Art* (Tucson: University of Arizona Press, 1978), 40.

2. Richard W. Payne, "Bone Flutes of the Anasazi," *Kiva* 56, no. 2 (1991): 166-67, 171-72.

3. Jay Miller, "Kokopelli," *Collected Papers in Honor of Florence Hawley Ellis,* ed. T. R. Frisbie, Archaeological Society of New Mexico Papers 2 (1975): 375.

4. Elsie Clews Parsons, "The Humpbacked Flute Player of the Southwest," *American Anthropologist* 40, no. 2 (1938): 337.

5. Polly Schaafsma, *Indian Rock Art of the Southwest*, 140; Frank Waters, "Kokopilau: The Humpbacked Flute Player," 20.

6. Etienne B. Renaud, "Kokopelli: A Study in Pueblo Mythology," *Southwestern Lore* 14, no. 2 (1948): 29.

7. Klaus F. Wellmann, "Kokopelli of Indian Paleology," 1679.

8. Elsie Clews Parsons, "The Humpbacked Flute Player," 337-38; Etienne B. Renaud, "Kokopelli: A Study in Pueblo Mythology," 39.

9. Polly Schaafsma, *Indian Rock Art of the Southwest,* 141.

10. Jesse Walter Fewkes, "Hopi Katcinas Drawn by Native Artists," *U.S. Bureau of American Ethnology, Twenty-first Annual Report for the Years 1899-1901* (Washington, D.C.: 1903): 110.

11. Campbell Grant, *Canyon de Chelly,* 70-72.
12. Joyce M. Alpert, "Kokopelli: A New Look at the Humpbacked Flute Player in Anasazi Rock Art," *American Indian Art Magazine* (Winter 1991): 51.
13. Campbell Grant, *Canyon de Chelly,* 207.
14. Christy G. Turner II, "Petrographs of the Glen Canyon Region," Museum of Northern Arizona Bulletin 38 (Glen Canyon Series 4, 1963): 22.
15. Jay Miller, "Kokopelli," 375.
16. Elsie Clews Parsons, "Some Aztec and Pueblo Parallels," *American Anthropologist* 35 (1933): 619-20; Carroll L. Riley, *The Frontier People: The Greater Southwest in the Protohistoric Period* (Albuquerque: University of New Mexico Press, 1987), 321-23.
17. Carroll L. Riley, *The Frontier People: The Greater Southwest in the Protohistoric Period,* 321.
18. Gladys A. Reichard, *Navajo Religion: A Study of Symbolism.* Vols. 1 and 2, Bollingen Series 18 (New York: Stratford Press, 1950), 443.
19. Leslie A. White, "The Acoma Indians," *U.S. Bureau of American Ethnology Annual Report, 1929-1930* 47 (Washington, D.C.: 1932): 162-64; Morris E. Opler, *An Apache Life-Way: The Economic, Social, and Religious Institutions of the Chiricahua Indians* (Chicago: University of Chicago Press, 1941), 267.
20. Ruth L. Bunzel, "Introduction to Zuni Ceremonialism," *U.S. Bureau of American Ethnology Annual Report, 1929-1930* 47 (Washington, D.C.: 1932): 864.
21. Lois Brill, "Kokopelli: Analysis of His Alleged Attributes and Suggestions Toward Alternate Identifications" (Master's thesis, University of New Mexico, Albuquerque, 1984).
22. Jesse Walter Fewkes, "Hopi Katcinas Drawn by Native Artists," 101-02.
23. Peter T. Furst, "Ethnographic Analogy in the Interpretation of West Mexican Art," in *The Archaeology of West Mexico,* ed. Betty Bell (Ajijic, Jalisco: West Mexican Society for Advanced Study, 1974), 137; Polly Schaafsma, *Indian Rock Art of the Southwest,* 136.
24. S. Linné, "Humpbacks in Ancient America," *Ethnos* 8 (1943): 170.
25. Lois Brill, "Kokopelli," 32.
26. G. B. Webb, "Tuberculosis," in *Clio Medico,* ed. E. G.

Krumbhaar (New York: Paul B. Hoeber, 1936), 7, 17; Klaus F. Wellmann, "Kokopelli of Indian Paleology," 1678-82; Joyce M. Alpert, "Kokopelli, a New Look," 50-57.

27. Emil W. Haury, *The Hohokam, Desert Farmers and Craftsmen* (Tucson: University of Arizona Press, 1976), 239.

28. Ibid., 240.

29. Ibid., 240.

30. Polly Schaafsma, Personal Communication, June 1993.

31. Harry L. Hadlock, "Ganaskidi—The Navajo Humpbacked Deity of the Largo," Papers of the Archaeological Society of New Mexico 5 (1980): 181; Gladys A. Reichard, *Navajo Religion*, 443.

32. Polly Schaafsma, *Indian Rock Art of the Southwest,* 317.

33. Gladys A. Reichard, *Navajo Religion,* 443.

34. Sally J. Cole, "Iconography and Symbolism in Basketmaker Rock Art," in *Rock Art of the Western Canyons,* ed. Jane S. Day, Paul D. Friedman, and Marcia J. Tate. Colorado Archaeological Society Memoir 3 (Denver Museum of Natural History, 1989), 79-81. Crooks and wooden sticks with crooked handles have fertility associations based on archaeological and historical ceremonial evidence. More than three hundred were removed from a room containing a high-status burial which was excavated at Pueblo Bonito in Chaco Canyon, New Mexico.

Section III: FLUTEPLAYER IMAGES IN ROCK ART

1. Polly Schaafsma, *Indian Rock Art of the Southwest* (Santa Fe and Albuquerque: School of American Research and University of New Mexico Press, 1980), 136.

2. Polly Schaafsma, *Rock Art in New Mexico* (Albuquerque: University of New Mexico Press, 1992), 91.

3. Carol Patterson-Rudolph, *Petroglyphs and Pueblo Myths of the Rio Grande* (Albuquerque, N.M.: Avanyu Publishing, Inc., 1990), 43-60. See Section V for complete account of myth.

4. The Cloud Blower is a small horn-shaped object as well as the name of the personage who uses it; native tobacco smoke was

blown through it in an attempt to attract rain clouds to the area.

5. Polly Schaafsma, *Rock Art in New Mexico*, 128.

6. Elsie Clews Parsons, *Pueblo Indian Religion* (Chicago: University of Chicago Press, 1939), 134, 333, 440-42, 456, 621-22, 646, 696-700, 880, 960.

7. Polly Schaafsma, *Rock Art in New Mexico*, 128.

8. Ibid., 93, 98.

9. Ibid., 128.

10. Ibid., 30.

11. Ibid., 27.

12. Ibid., 10.

13. M. Jane Young, *Signs from the Ancestors* (Albuquerque: University of New Mexico Press, 1988), 141.

14. Ibid., 250.

15. Ibid., 67.

16. David P. Fletcher, Canyon de Chelly section in *Canyon Country Prehistoric Rock Art*, ed. F. A. Barnes (Salt Lake City, Utah: Wasatch Publishers, Inc., 1982), 192.

17. Campbell Grant, *Canyon de Chelly: Its People and Rock Art* (Tucson: The University of Arizona Press, 1978), 159-60.

18. Polly Schaafsma, *Indian Rock Art of the Southwest*, 111.

19. Campbell Grant, *Canyon de Chelly*, 183.

20. Ibid., 201.

21. Ibid., 189.

22. Ibid., 193, 195.

23. Peter J. Pilles, Jr., "The Sinagua: Ancient People of the Flagstaff Region," in *Exploration: Annual Bulletin of the School of American Research*, ed. David Grant Noble (Santa Fe, N.M.: School of American Research, 1987), 3-11.

24. Polly Schaafsma, "Rock Art at Wupatki: Pots, Textiles, Glyphs," in *Exploration: Annual Bulletin of the School of American Research*, ed. David Grant Noble (Santa Fe, N.M.: School of American Research, 1987), 21-27.

25. Polly Schaafsma, *Indian Rock Art of the Southwest,* 131-32.

26. Ibid., 109-19.

27. From paper presented by Steven J. Manning at the Utah Rock Art Research Association Symposium held at Green River, Utah, September 5-7, 1992.

28. Kenneth B. Castleton, *Petroglyphs and Pictographs of Utah.* Volume 2, *The South, Central, West, and Northwest* (Salt Lake City: Utah Museum of Natural History, 1979), 249.

29. Ibid., 326.
30. Polly Schaafsma, *Indian Rock Art of the Southwest*, 61-72.
31. Polly Schaafsma, Personal Communication, August 1993.
32. Sally J. Cole, *Legacy on Stone: Rock Art of the Colorado Plateau and Four Corners Region* (Boulder, Colo.: Johnson Books, 1990), 157-64.
33. Ibid., 130.
34. Helen Sloan Daniels, Pictographs, Appendix A, in *Basketmaker II Sites Near Durango, Colorado*, by Earl H. Morris and Robert F. Burgh, in Carnegie Institution of Washington Publication 604 (Washington, D.C.: Carnegie Institution, 1954), 88, fig. 111.
35. Gary Matlock, Personal Communication, June 1992. Matlock, of Durango, states that both Basketmaker II and Basketmaker III remains were found in the valley below the shelters.
36. Sally J. Cole, *Legacy on Stone*, 199-200.
37. Sally J. Cole and Danni L. Langdon, West-Central Colorado Area section in *Canyon Country Prehistoric Rock Art*, ed. F. A. Barnes (Salt Lake City, Utah: Wasatch Publishers, Inc., 1982), 279.
38. Sally J. Cole, *Legacy on Stone*, 194.
39. Polly Schaafsma, *Indian Rock Art of the Southwest*, 21.
40. Kenneth B. Castleton, *Petroglyphs and Pictographs of Utah*. Volume 1: *The East and Northeast* (Salt Lake City: Utah Museum of Natural History, 1984), 74.
41. Polly Schaafsma, *Indian Rock Art of the Southwest*, 183-87.
42. Polly Schaafsma, site report for Museum of New Mexico, 1971.
43. Polly Schaafsma, *Indian Rock Art of the Southwest*, 221.
44. Emil W. Haury, *The Hohokam, Desert Farmers and Craftsmen* (Tucson: University of Arizona Press, 1976), 332, 337.

Section IV: FLUTEPLAYER IMAGES IN CERAMICS AND KIVA MURALS

1. Watson Smith, "Kiva Mural Decorations at Awatovi and Kawaika-a," Papers of the Peabody Museum of Archaeology and Ethnology 37 (1952): 220.
2. Marjorie F. Lambert, "A Kokopelli Effigy Pitcher from

Northwestern New Mexico," *American Antiquity* 32, no. 3 (1967): 398-400.

3. Marjorie F. Lambert, *Paa-ko, Archaeological Chronicle of an Indian Village in North Central New Mexico,* School of American Research Monograph 19 (1954): fig. 16d.

4. Emil W. Haury, *The Hohokam, Desert Farmers and Craftsmen* (Tucson: University of Arizona Press, 1976), 240.

5. Ibid., 240, fig. 12.91,c.

6. Constance S. Silver, "The Mural Paintings from the Kiva at LA 17360: Report on Initial Treatment for Their Preservation," in *Prehistoric Adaptive Strategies in the Chaco Canyon Region, Northwestern New Mexico.* Vol. 2: *Site Reports,* ed. Alan H. Simmons, Navajo Nation Papers in Anthropology 9 (1982): 715.

7. Watson Smith, "Mural Decorations at Awatovi," 19.

8. Constance S. Silver, "Mural Paintings from the Kiva at LA 17360," 715.

9. Clyde Kluckhohn, "The Excavations of Bc 51 Rooms and Kivas," University of New Mexico Bulletin 345, Anthropological Series 3, no. 2 (1939): 43.

10. Watson Smith, "Mural Decorations at Awatovi," 299.

11. Frederick Lange et al., *Yellow Jacket: A Four Corners Anasazi Ceremonial Center* (Boulder, Colo.: Johnson Books, 1986), 32.

12. Bruce A. Bradley, "Architectural Petroglyphs at Sand Canyon Pueblo (5MT765) Southwestern Colorado," *Kiva* 54, no. 2 (1989): 158-59.

Section V: MYTHS AND STORIES

1. Polly Schaafsma and Curtis F. Schaafsma, "Origins of the Pueblo Katchina Cult," *American Antiquity* 39, no. 4 (1974): 535-45.

2. Polly Schaafsma, "Kachinas in Rock Art," *Journal of New World Archaeology* 4, no.2 (1981): 30.

3. Florence Hawley, "Kokopelli of the Prehistoric Southwestern Pueblo Pantheon," *American Anthropologist* 39 (1937): 644-46.

4. Joyce M. Alpert, "Kokopelli: A New Look at the Humpbacked Flute Player in Anasazi Rock Art," *American Indian Art Magazine* (Winter 1991): 55.

5. Mischa Titiev, "The Story of Kokopele," *American Anthropologist* 41, no. 1 (1939): 95.
6. Ibid., 96.
7. Ibid., 91-94.
8. Ibid., 94-95.
9. M. Jane Young, *Signs from the Ancestors* (Albuquerque: University of New Mexico Press, 1988), 141.
10. Ibid., 142.
11. Klaus F. Wellmann, "Kokopelli of Indian Paleology: Hunchbacked Rain Priest, Hunting Magician, and Don Juan of the Old Southwest," *Journal of the American Medical Association* 212 (1970): 1682; Campbell Grant, *Rock Art of the American Indian* (third printing; Dillon, Colo.: Vistabooks, 1992), 61.
12. Dennis Tedlock, *Finding the Center: Narrative Poetry of the Zuni Indians* (Lincoln: University of Nebraska Press, 1972), 118-31.
13. Ibid., 127.
14. Carol Patterson-Rudolph, *Petroglyphs and Pueblo Myths of the Rio Grande* (Albuquerque, N.M.: Avanyu Publishing Inc., 1990), 43-51.
15. Elsie Clews Parsons, "The Humpbacked Flute Player of the Southwest," *American Anthropologist* 40, no. 2 (1938): 337.
16. Ibid., 338.
17. Klaus F. Wellmann, "The Indomitable Hump-back Returns," *La Pintura* 1, no.2 (1974): 2, 4.
18. Ibid., 6.
19. Ibid., 6.
20. Ibid., 4.
21. Ibid., 6.

References

Alpert, Joyce M. "Kokopelli: A New Look at the Humpbacked Flute Player in Anasazi Rock Art." *American Indian Art Magazine* (Winter 1991): 49-57.

Barnes, F. A., ed. *Canyon Country Prehistoric Rock Art*. Salt Lake City, Utah: Wasatch Publishers, Inc., 1982.

Blumenschein, Helen G. *Selected Petroglyphs in Rio Arriba County*. Boulder, Colo.: Pruett Press, 1973.

Boyd, Douglas K., and Bobbie Ferguson. *Tewa Rock Art in the Black Mesa Region*. Amarillo, Tex.: U.S. Department of the Interior, Bureau of Reclamation, Southwest Region, 1988.

Bradley, Bruce A. "Architectural Petroglyphs at Sand Canyon Pueblo (5MT765), Southwestern Colorado." *Kiva* 54, no.2 (1989): 153-61.

Brill, Lois. "Kokopelli: Analysis of His Alleged Attributes and Suggestions Toward Alternate Identifications." Master's thesis, University of New Mexico, Albuquerque, 1984.

Brody, J. J. *Mimbres Painted Pottery.* Santa Fe and Albuquerque: School of American Research and University of New Mexico Press, 1977.

_____. *Anasazi and Pueblo Painting.* Albuquerque: University of New Mexico Press, 1991.

Bruggmann, Maximilien, and Sylvio Acatos. *Die Pueblos.* Zurich: U. Baer Verlag, 1989.

Bunzel, Ruth L. "Introduction to Zuni Ceremonialism." *U.S. Bureau of American Ethnology Annual Report, 1929-1930* 47 (1932): 467-544.

Castleton, Kenneth B. *Petroglyphs and Pictographs of Utah.* Volume 1: *The East and Northeast.* Salt Lake City: Utah Museum of Natural History, 1984.

_____. *Petroglyphs and Pictographs of Utah.* Volume 2: *The South, Central, West, and Northwest.* Salt Lake City: Utah Museum of Natural History, 1987.

Christensen, Don D. "Scratched Glyphs in Arizona: A Reevaluation." In *Rock Art Papers* 9. Edited by Ken Hedges. *San Diego Museum Papers* 8 (1992): 101-10.

Cole, Sally J. "Iconography and Symbolism in Basketmaker Rock Art." In *Rock Art of the Western Canyons.* Edited by Jane S. Day, Paul D. Friedman, and Marcia J. Tate. Colorado Archaeological Society Memoir 3: 59-85. Denver, Colo.: Denver Museum of Natural History, 1989a.

_____. "Katsina Iconography in Homol'ovi Rock Art." *Kiva* 54, no. 3 (1989b): 313-29.

_____. *Legacy on Stone: Rock Art of the Colorado Plateau and Four Corners Region.* Boulder, Colo.: Johnson Books, 1990.

Cutler, Hugh C. "Medicine Men and the Preservation of a Relict Gene in Maize." *Journal of Heredity* 35 (1944): 291-94.

Daniels, Helen Sloan. Pictographs. In *Basketmaker II Sites Near*

Durango, Colorado, Appendix A, by Earl H. Morris and Robert F. Burgh. Carnegie Institution of Washington Publication 604 (1954).

Dedrick, Philip. "An Analysis of the Human Figure Motif on North American Prehistoric Painted Pottery." Master's thesis, University of New Mexico, Albuquerque, 1958.

Di Peso, Charles C. *Casas Grandes—A Fallen Trading Center of the Gran Chichimeca*. Dragoon, Ariz.: Amerind Foundation, 1974.

Durham, Dorothy. "Petroglyphs at Mesa de los Padillas," *El Palacio* 62 (1955).

Fallon, Denise P. "An Archaeological Investigation of the Petroglyphs at the Waterflow Site, LA 8970, San Juan County, New Mexico." Laboratory of Anthropology Note 135. Santa Fe: Museum of New Mexico, 1979.

Fewkes, Jesse Walter. "Hopi Katcinas Drawn by Native Artists." *U.S. Bureau of American Ethnology, Twenty-first Annual Report for the Years 1899-1901* (1903): 3-126.

Foster, Gene. "Petrographic Art in Glen Canyon." *Plateau* 27 (1954): 6-18.

Furst, Peter T. "Ethnographic Analogy in the Interpretation of West Mexican Art." In *The Archaeology of West Mexico*. Edited by Betty Bell. Ajijic, Jalisco, Mex.: West Mexican Society for Advanced Study, 1974.

Grant, Campbell. *Canyon de Chelly: Its People and Rock Art*. Tucson: University of Arizona Press, 1978.

_____. *Rock Art of the American Indian*. Third Printing. Dillon, Colo.: Vistabooks, 1992.

_____, James W. Baird, and J. Kenneth Pringle. *Rock Drawings of the Coso Range*. Ridgecrest, Calif.: Maturango Press, 1968.

Hadlock, Harry L. "Ganaskidi—The Navajo Humpback Deity of the Largo." Papers of the Archaeological Society of New Mexico 5 (1980): 179-210.

Haury, Emil W. *The Hohokam, Desert Farmers and Craftsmen.* Tucson: University of Arizona Press, 1976.

Hawley, Florence. "Kokopelli of the Prehistoric Southwestern Pueblo Pantheon." *American Anthropologist* 39 (1937): 644-46.

Hayes, Alden C. "The Archaeological Survey of Wetherill Mesa." National Park Service, Archaeological Research Series 7-A. Washington, D.C., 1964.

Hibben, Frank C. "Excavation of the Riana Ruin and Chama Valley Survey." University of New Mexico Bulletin, Anthropological Series 2, no. 1 (1937): 1-60, Plate XIIIa.

Johnson, Clay. "Clay's Tablet (Barrier Canyon)." *Utah Rock Art* 7 (1990): ii. Edited by Bonnie L. Morris. Salt Lake City: Utah Rock Art Research Association.

Judd, Neil M. "The Material Culture of Pueblo Bonito," *Smithsonian Miscellaneous Collections* 124. Washington, D.C.: Smithsonian Institution (1954): 200.

Kidder, Alfred Vincent, and Samuel J. Guernsey. "Archeological Explorations in Northeastern Arizona." U.S. Bureau of American Ethnology Bulletin 65. Washington, D.C., 1919.

Kluckhohn, Clyde. "The Excavations of Bc 51 Rooms and Kivas." University of New Mexico Bulletin 345, Anthropological Series 3, no.2 (1939): 30-48.

Lambert, Marjorie F. "Paa-ko, Archaeological Chronicle of an Indian Village in North Central New Mexico." School of American Research Monograph 19. Santa Fe, N.M.: School of American Research, 1954.

_____. " A Kokopelli Effigy Pitcher from Northwestern New Mexico." *American Antiquity* 32, no. 3 (1967): 398-401.

Lange, Frederick, Nancy Mahaney, Joe Ben Wheat, and Mark L. Chenault. *Yellow Jacket: A Four Corners Anasazi Ceremonial Center*. Boulder, Colo.: Johnson Books, 1986.

Linné, S. "Humpbacks in Ancient America." *Ethnos* 8 (1943): 161- 86.

Manning, Steven J. "The Lobed-Circle Image in the Basket-maker Petroglyphs of Southeastern Utah." *Utah Rock Art* 10 (1990): 149-208. Edited by Nina Bowen. Salt Lake City: Utah Rock Art Research Association.

Marshall, Michael P., and Henry J. Walt. *Rio Abajo: Prehistory and History of a Rio Grande Province*. Santa Fe: New Mexico Historic Preservation Program, 1984.

Miller, Jay. "Kokopelli." *Collected Papers in Honor of Florence Hawley Ellis*. Edited by T. R. Frisbie. Archaeological Society of New Mexico Papers 2 (1975): 371-80.

Neary, John. "Kokopelli Kitsch." *Archaeology* (July-August 1992): 76.

Noble, David Grant, ed. *New Light on Chaco Canyon*. Santa Fe, N.M.: School of American Research Press, 1984.

Opler, Morris E. *An Apache Life-Way: The Economic, Social, and Religious Institutions of the Chiricahua Indians*. Chicago: University of Chicago Press, 1941.

Parsons, Elsie Clews. "Some Aztec and Pueblo Parallels." *American Anthropologist* 35 (1933): 611-31.

_____. "The Humpbacked Flute Player of the Southwest." *American Anthropologist* 40, no.2 (1938): 337-38.

_____. *Pueblo Indian Religion*. Chicago: University of Chicago Press, 1939.

Patterson, Alex. *A Field Guide to Rock Art Symbols of the Greater Southwest*. Boulder, Colo.: Johnson Books, 1992.

Patterson-Rudolph, Carol. *Petroglyphs and Pueblo Myths of the Rio Grande*. Albuquerque, N.M.: Avanyu Publishing, Inc., 1990.

Payne, Richard W. "Indian Flutes of the Southwest." *Journal of the American Musical Instrument Society* 15 (1989): 5-31.

_____. "Bone Flutes of the Anasazi." *Kiva* 56, no.2 (1991): 165-77.

Pilles, Peter J., Jr. "The Sinagua: Ancient People of the Flagstaff Region." In *Exploration: Annual Bulletin of the School of American Research*. Edited by David Grant Noble. Santa Fe, N.M.: School of American Research, 1987.

Reichard, Gladys A. *Navajo Religion: A Study of Symbolism*. 2 vols. Bollingen Series 18. New York: Stratford Press, 1950.

Renaud, Etienne B. "Kokopelli: A Study in Pueblo Mythology." *Southwestern Lore* 14, no. 2 (1948): 25-40.

Riley, Carroll L. *The Frontier People: The Greater Southwest in the Protohistoric Period*. Albuquerque: University of New Mexico Press, 1987.

Riley, Robert A. Rock Art at La Bajada Mesa, New Mexico. Unpublished manuscript, 1973.

Roberts, Frank H. H., Jr. "The Village of the Great Kivas on the Zuni Reservation." U.S. Bureau of American Ethnology Bulletin 111 (1932).

Russell, Sharman Apt. *Songs of the Fluteplayer*. Reading, Mass.: Addison-Wesley Publishing Co., 1991.

Schaafsma, Polly. "Rock Art in the Navajo Reservoir District." *Museum of New Mexico Papers in Anthropology* 7. Santa Fe: Museum of New Mexico Press, 1963.

_____. "A Survey of Tsegi Canyon Rock Art," unpublished manuscript, National Park Service Region 3, Santa Fe, N.M. (1966): Fig. 28.

_____. "The Rock Art of Utah." Papers of the Peabody Museum of Archaeology and Ethnology 65. Cambridge, Mass.: Harvard University Press, 1971.

_____. *Rock Art in New Mexico*. Albuquerque: University of New Mexico Press, 1975.

_____. *Indian Rock Art of the Southwest*. Santa Fe and Albuquerque, N.M.: School of American Research and University of New Mexico Press, 1980.

_____. "Kachinas in Rock Art." *Journal of New World Archaeology* 4, no.2 (1981): 25-32.

_____. "Anasazi Rock Art in Tsegi Canyon and Canyon de Chelly: A View Behind the Image." In *Exploration: Annual Bulletin of the School of American Research*. Edited by David Grant Noble. Santa Fe. N.M.: School of American Research, 1986.

_____. "Rock Art at Wupatki: Pots, Textiles, Glyphs." In *Exploration: Annual Bulletin of the School of American Research*. Edited by David Grant Noble. Santa Fe, N.M.: School of American Research, 1987.

_____. *Rock Art in New Mexico*. Santa Fe: Museum of New Mexico Press, 1992.

_____. Personal Communications, June and August 1993.

Schaafsma, Polly, and Curtis F. Schaafsma. "Origins of the Pueblo Katchina Cult." *American Antiquity* 39, no.4 (1974): 535-45.

Shuler, Linda Lay. *She Who Remembers*. New York: Penguin Books, 1988.

Silver, Constance S. "The Mural Paintings from the Kiva at LA 17360: Report on Initial Treatment for Their Preservation." In *Prehistoric Adaptive Strategies in the Chaco Canyon Region, Northwestern New Mexico*. Vol. 2, *Site Reports*. Edited by Alan H. Simmons. Navajo Nation Papers in Anthropology 9. Window Rock, Ariz.: Navajo Nation Cultural Resource Management Program, 1982.

Sims, Agnes C. *San Cristobal Petroglyphs*. Santa Fe, N.M.: Southwestern Editions, 1950.

Smith, Howard N., Jr. A Survey and Stylistic Analysis of Rock Art in the San Juan Basin. Master's thesis, Eastern New Mexico University, Portales, 1974.

Smith, Watson. "Kiva Mural Decorations at Awatovi and Kawaika-a." Papers of the Peabody Museum of Archaeology and Ethnology 37. Cambridge, Mass.: Harvard University Press, 1952.

Steed, Paul. "Rock Art in Chaco Canyon." *The Artifact* 18, no.3 (1980): 143.

Steward, Julian H. "Archeological Reconnaissance of Southern Utah." U.S. Bureau of American Ethnology Bulletin 128. Washington, D.C., 1941.

_____. "Petroglyphs of California and Adjoining States." *University of California Publications in American Archaeology and Ethnology* 24, no. 2 (1929): 47-238.

Tedlock, Dennis. *Finding the Center: Narrative Poetry of the Zuni Indians*. Lincoln: University of Nebraska Press, 1972.

Titiev, Mischa. "The Story of Kokopele." *American Anthropologist* 41, no.1 (1939): 91-98.

Towler, Solala. *Cocopeli Stories*. Deadwood, Oreg.: Coyote Press, 1982.

Trask, Lance. "Ancient Billboards: The Rock Art of the Lower Jemez Mountains." ARM Survey No. 41167. Santa Fe National Forest and the Maxwell Museum, 1992.

Turner, Christy G., II. "Petrographs of the Glen Canyon Region." Museum of Northern Arizona Bulletin 38 (Glen Canyon Series 4), Flagstaff, Ariz., 1963.

Vuncannon, Delcie H. "Grand Gulch: Southeastern Utah's Picture Gallery." In *American Indian Rock Art*, vol. 2, 5-18. Edited by Kay Sutherland. El Paso, Tex.: El Paso Archaeological Society, Inc., 1976.

_____. "Petroglyphs in Johns Canyon, Utah." In *American Indian Rock Art*, vol.4, 156-69. Edited by Ernest Snyder, A. J. Bock, and Frank Bock. El Toro, Calif.: American Rock Art Research Association, 1978.

Warner, Jesse E. "Transformation II: Man to Bird." In *Utah Rock Art,* vol. 9, 31-41. Edited by Nina Bowen. Salt Lake City: Utah Rock Art Research Association, 1989.

_____. "An Examination of Double Entities—The Application of Symbolism." In *Utah Rock Art,* vol. 7, no. 5, 1- 19. Edited by Bonnie L. Morris. Salt Lake City: Utah Rock Art Research Association, 1990.

Waters, Frank. "Kokopilau: The Humpbacked Flute Player." *Shaman's Drum* 10 (Fall 1987): 17-20.

Webb, G. B. "Tuberculosis." In *Clio Medica*. Edited by E. G. Krumbhaar. New York: Paul B. Hoeber, Inc., 1936.

Wellmann, Klaus F. "Kokopelli of Indian Paleology: Hunchbacked Rain Priest, Hunting Magician, and Don Juan of the Old Southwest." *Journal of the American Medical Association* 212 (1970): 1678-82.

_____. "The Indomitable Hump-back Returns." *La Pintura* 1, no. 2 (1974): 2, 4.

_____. *North American Indian Rock Art*. Graz, Austria: Akademische Druk- und Verlagsanstalt, 1979.

White, Leslie A. "The Acoma Indians." *U.S. Bureau of American Ethnology Annual Report, 1929-1930*. Washington, D.C., 1932.

Williams, Terry Tempest. "Kokopelli's Return," *From the Canyons* (Summer 1989): 17.

Young, M. Jane. *Signs from the Ancestors*. Albuquerque: University of New Mexico Press, 1988.

Young, John V. *Kokopelli: Casanova of the Cliff Dwellers*. Palmer Lake, Colo.: Filter Press, 1990.

Zwinger, Ann. *Wind in the Rock*. Tucson: University of Arizona Press, 1986.

Glossary

ABAJO-LA SAL STYLE. An early Anasazi rock art style combining characteristics of other Colorado Plateau styles (Barrier Canyon, San Juan Basketmaker, and Fremont). This style is essentially limited to rock art sites in the Abajo Mountains (Utah), canyons in the Moab (Utah) area, and to a portion of the Dolores River drainage in Colorado.

ABSTRACT STYLE. Nonrepresentational rock art attributed to hunter-gatherers and occurring primarily in the Great Basin, the Chihuahuan Desert, and along the Rio Grande in northern New Mexico, extending into southern Colorado and northeastern New Mexico. This style consists of various combinations of dots, parallel and wavy lines, zigzags, circles, and amorphous components. The geometric motif is a different sort of abstract element found in later rock art, especially in the Anasazi and Mogollon regions and in ceramic decoration.

ANASAZI. Navajo word meaning "Ancient Ones." Term used in referring to the Basketmaker and Pueblo periods of the prehistoric culture of southern Utah, southwestern Colorado, northern New Mexico and Arizona, and the southern tip of Nevada. The Anasazi are considered to be ancestors of most modern Pueblo people.

ANTHROPOMORPH. In rock art, an element of human or humanoid form. An anthropomorphic style is one in which this type of element is dominant.

ARCHAIC CULTURE. Usually referred to as Western Archaic in the Southwest, this was a culture of hunters and gatherers which commenced around the middle of the sixth millennium B.C. in that region. Their rock art was representational as well as abstract.

AWANYU. Horned or feathered serpent depicted frequently in rock art, especially in the Anasazi region. The awanyu is associated with moisture sources, such as springs or streams. It apparently has Mexican antecedents and, perhaps, an ideological connection with the god Quetzalcoatl.

BARRIER CANYON (ANTHROPOMORPHIC) STYLE. Named for its type-site, Barrier Creek in Horseshoe Canyon, Utah (Canyonlands National Park), this style of the Archaic anthropomorphic tradition emphasizes elongated human or supernatural figures, often appearing in groups of two or more. Arms and legs are usually minimally depicted or are missing entirely; large, "goggle" eyes are frequently the only facial features. These figures are usually painted with a dark red pigment.

BASKETMAKER PERIOD. Pre-Pueblo period of the Anasazi cultural tradition extending from at least as early as the third century B.C. to around A.D. 700. This period is separated into Basketmaker II and Basketmaker III subdivisions; Basketmaker I is now generally considered to be part of the later Western Archaic tradition. The earliest Anasazi rock art is that of the Basketmaker IIPeriod.

CARBON 14 (RADIOCARBON). Radioactive isotope of carbon with mass number 14, used by archaeologists to date organic material. Abbreviation: C-14.

CAVE VALLEY STYLE. Found at late Basketmaker/early Pueblo sites in the Virgin Kayenta area of southwestern Utah and adjacent parts of Arizona, this style is characterized by human figures or supernaturals usually composed of triangular elements and normally occurring as pictographs in a wide range of colors.

CLASSIC VERNAL STYLE. See UINTA.

FREMONT. Prehistoric culture region covering most of Utah (except the southeastern corner) and narrow, adjacent portions of Nevada, Wyoming, and Colorado. This culture was involved in an exchange of rock art symbolism with the Anasazi to the south. Approximate date range: A.D. 400 to A.D. 1350, with a possible terminal date around A.D. 1500. The Fremont area has been divided into five culture regions, each with its particular rock art style: Sevier, Parowan, Great Salt Lake, Uinta, and San Rafael, the latter being subdivided by Polly Schaafsma into the Southern San Rafael and Northern San Rafael rock art styles.

GOBERNADOR PHASE. Navajo culture period (about A.D. 1696 to A.D. 1775) represented in rock art by petroglyphs and pictographs found in the Gobernador District along the upper San Juan River drainage in northwestern New Mexico and adjacent region of Colorado. The iconography of the Gobernador Representational Style includes *ye'i* figures (supernatural beings from Navajo mythology), shield bearers, cloud terraces, birds, animals, corn plants, and planetaria.

GREAT SALT LAKE. Cultural subdivision of the Fremont with a date range of approximately A.D. 400 to A.D. 1350. The concomitant rock art style includes horned anthropomorphs, abstract elements, and red-painted, triangular anthropomorphs, the latter figures constituting the Western Utah Painted Style.

HOHOKAM. Prehistoric desert culture concentrated in the drainage system of the Gila and Salt rivers of southern Arizona. Date range: about A.D. 300 for the beginning of the initial (Pioneer) period to about A.D. 1450 for the end of the terminal (Classic) period.

ICONOGRAPHY. In rock art, the science of the description and study of pictorial depictions and symbolism; a collection of representations.

INSECTIFORM. Representation (in rock art, etc.) of insect and insectlike forms. The fluteplayer is occasionally depicted in locust, ant, or other (often unidentifiable) insect shape.

JORNADA STYLE. Rock art style of the eastern regions (Mimbres and Jornada) of Mogollon culture. Jornada Style rock art has iconographic connections with Mexico, especially in the frequent depictions of horned and/or plumed serpents, the impressive variety of masks, and the many portrayals of a goggle-eyed, abstract figure (the latter apparently analogous to Tlaloc, the Mexican rain god).

MIMBRES. Cultural subdivision of the eastern (or Desert) Mogollon, focused on the Mimbres River Valley in southwestern New Mexico. Mimbres pottery is famous for the charm and sophistication of its imagery as well as for the ingenious manner in which elements are arranged. Anthropomorphs and animals are often depicted in rock art of the area with decorative interior ornamentation similar to that found on Mimbres pottery.

MOGOLLON CULTURE. Prehistoric cultural entity which occupied much of southern New Mexico and southeastern Arizona; it is separated into five subdivisions. Approximate dates for the western (Mountain) Mogollon are 100 B.C. to A.D. 1350; for the eastern (Desert) Mogollon A.D. 800 to A.D. 1400.

MOGOLLON RED. Style characterized by small, red paintings of simple anthropomorphs, fish, zigzags, circles, multiple dots or short lines, and bird tracks. Mogollon Red pictographs occur in southwestern New Mexico (especially in the Mogollon Mountains and nearby drainages) and in a limited area of southeastern Arizona. Agreement has not been reached as to the beginning date for this style, but it extended at least to about A.D.. 1300.

NORTHERN SAN RAFAEL. Rock art style associated with the San Rafael cultural subdivision of the Fremont tradition, dated approximately A.D. 700 to A.D. 1200. Animals and abstract elements dominate the rock art of the Northern San Rafael Style; the type-site is Nine Mile Canyon, Utah.

PALEO-INDIAN PERIOD. The earliest cultural remains of the Southwest are from the Paleo-Indian tradition dated prior to 5500 B.C. This was a primitive hunter-gatherer culture with a low density population, involved in the pursuit of large mammals, mostly now extinct. Southwestern rock art of this period is considered to be minimal or perhaps nonexistent.

PAROWAN. Cultural subdivision of the Fremont tradition, dated about A.D. 900 to A.D. 1300. Abstract elements predominate in Parowan Style rock art; however, Fremont anthropomorphs are also depicted. The type-site is near Parowan, Utah.

PETROGLYPH. Rock art created by various techniques: pecking, abrading, scratching, and incising—usually by employing a hard, stone implement on a patinated rock surface.

PICTOGRAPH. Rock art created by painting or drawing on the rock surface which is normally protected from the elements by an overhang or cavate location. Natural pigments were employed, such as hematite, charcoal, gypsum, colored clays, and vegetable dyes. Water, seed oils, egg whites, and possibly blood or urine were used as binders. Pigment was applied by the fingers, by sticks, and by a variety of natural brushes.

POLYCHROME STYLE. In rock art, a pictograph style in which multiple colors are employed, as in the Chihuahuan Polychrome Abstract Style (Western Archaic).

PUEBLO PERIOD. The later cultural divisions of the Anasazi tradition, commencing with Pueblo I (aboveground masonry villages, transitional rock art styles—ca. A.D. 700 to A.D. 900), and ending with Pueblo V (historic Spanish, Mexican, and Anglo-American—A.D. 1540 to the present).

REPRESENTATIONAL STYLE. In southwestern rock art, this style emphasizes life-forms (anthropomorphs, birds, quadrupeds, snakes, plants) and items in daily or ritual use. Such elements are usually stylized in varying degrees. Examples of this style are the Barrier Canyon and Cave Valley styles.

RESERVE PETROGLYPH STYLE. Belonging to the western (Mountain) Mogollon cultural tradition and located primarily in the San Francisco-Tularosa River drainages in Catron County, New Mexico, this style dates from about A.D. 1000 to A.D. 1300. Some elements typical of this style are animal tracks, human footprints, stick-figure anthropomorphs, fluteplayers, quadrupeds, lizards, outlined crosses, and various abstract designs.

RIO GRANDE STYLE. Commencing around A.D. 1300, this rock art style was heavily influenced by the Jornada Style to the south, was concentrated in the northern Rio Grande drainage, and extended to the western Pueblos. This style has persisted well into the historic period, continuing to this day at Zuni. Characteristic elements are anthropomorphs with rectangular bodies, large feet, and well-defined knees and calves; shields and shield figures; humpbacked fluteplayers; masks; kachina figures; mammals; birds; snakes; cloud terraces; four-pointed stars; and ritual participants.

SAN JUAN ANTHROPOMORPHIC STYLE (BASKETMAKER II PERIOD). This rock art style (probably shamanic in nature) is characterized by large, broad-shouldered anthropomorphic figures, usually depicted in groups or pairs; they are often very elaborate, with various types of headgear, necklaces, and earrings. Hands and feet with downward-directed fingers and toes are common. This style is concentrated in the San Juan River drainage, the type-site being located near the mouth of Butler Wash, Utah.

SAN RAFAEL STYLE. See SOUTHERN SAN RAFAEL, NORTHERN SAN RAFAEL.

SEVIER. Cultural subdivision of the Fremont tradition, dated approximately A.D. 800 to A.D. 1250 and occurring mainly in the Sevier River drainage of west-central Utah. Sevier Style A rock art is typified by a preponderance of quadrupeds (primarily mountain sheep), birds, snakes, handprints, and tracks, with fewer anthropomorphic representations than elsewhere in Fremont rock art.

SHALAKO. A guardian/rain-bringing kachina characterized by a long, tubular "beak." This kachina, six of which appear at the Coming of the Gods ceremony at Zuni near the winter solstice, is found in petroglyphs from the Little Colorado to the Rio Grande, but is best known in the western part of this region. Zuni-type shalakos were portrayed in the rock art of the Upper Rio Grande Valley in the fourteenth and fifteenth centuries A.D. There is also a Hopi Shalako kachina.

SIKYATKI POLYCHROME. Hopi pottery style dating from the fifteenth through the seventeenth centuries A.D. and named for a long-abandoned Hopi village on First Mesa. This complex painting style is related to that of kiva mural paintings found in the area.

SINAGUA. Prehistoric culture centered around Flagstaff, Arizona, from about the seventh century A.D. to the fourteenth century. Sinagua ("waterless" in Spanish) culture was heavily influenced by the neighboring Anasazi, Hohokam, and Mogollon. Rock art iconography of the Sinagua is similar to that of the Kayenta (Western) Anasazi, but places more emphasis on elaborate abstract designs which often contain beautiful geometric elements.

SOUTHERN SAN RAFAEL. Rock art style associated with the San Rafael cultural subdivision of the Fremont, dated approximately A.D. 700 to A.D. 1200. The type-sites for this style are along the Fremont River in Capitol Reef National Park (Utah). Broad-shouldered human figures in elaborate ceremonial regalia are characteristic of this style, as are shield bearers and mountain sheep, the latter often quite large.

TEWA. Tewa-speaking province of the Pueblo region, divided into northern and southern sections, the former comprising an area extending from upper White Rock Canyon (New Mexico) to the Rio Grande Gorge north of Velarde, New Mexico, and including Santa Fe. The Southern Tewa (or Tano) Province is centered around the Galisteo Basin northeast of Albuquerque.

TOMPIRO DISTRICT. Division of the Piro Province, the southern-most Rio Grande Pueblo area, located on or near mesas east of the Rio Grande and south of Albuquerque. Also called Mountain Piro.

UINTA. Cultural subdivision of the Fremont tradition, dated from before A.D. 800 to about A.D. 950. Type-sites for the Classic Vernal Style of Uinta Fremont rock art are located in the Ashley Creek/Dry Fork valleys near Vernal, Utah, and in Dinosaur National Monument (Colorado and Utah). Uinta Fremont rock art is also found in Brown's Park and Glade Park in northwestern Colorado. The Classic Vernal Style is typified by large (perhaps shamanic) anthropomorphs often depicted in groups, wearing elaborate ceremonial regalia, and occasionally carrying shields or masks. These panels are usually composed of petroglyphs executed in various techniques, but are often also painted. Some other elements of this style are spirals, circles, quadrupeds, lizards, and fluteplayers.

(CLASSIC) VERNAL STYLE. See UINTA.

VIRGIN KAYENTA. Branch of the Anasazi cultural tradition located in southwestern Utah and a small adjacent portion of Nevada, a region abandoned by its prehistoric inhabitants in the twelfth century A.D. The rock art of the Virgin Kayenta area has a more restricted iconography than that found in neighboring Anasazi areas to the east. Also, fluteplayers as well as pottery and textile motifs are less abundant; mountain sheep and deer with elaborate antlers are favorite subjects.

WESTERN ARCHAIC. See ARCHAIC CULTURE.

WESTERN UTAH PAINTED STYLE. See GREAT SALT LAKE.

ZOOMORPH. In rock art iconography, an element representing an animal or animal-like form. A zoomorphic style is one which strongly emphasizes such forms.

Appendix

THE MANY GUISES AND RELATIONS

Figure A-1
Petroglyph, north of
Española,
New Mexico.

Figure A-2
Pictograph,
Uncompahgre River
drainage, Colorado.
After Cole, 1990.

Figure A-3
Petroglyph,
La Cieneguilla,
New Mexico.

Figure A-4
Kokopelli (?) motif on
Mimbres bowl,
southern New Mexico.
After Brody, 1977.

FLUTEPLAYER IMAGES IN ROCK ART

Figure A-5
Petroglyph, near
Holbrook, Arizona.

Figure A-6
Petroglyph,
La Cieneguilla,
New Mexico.

Figure A-7
Petroglyph,
La Cieneguilla,
New Mexico.

Figure A-8
Petroglyphs,
La Cieneguilla,
New Mexico.

Figure A-9
Petroglyphs,
La Cieneguilla,
New Mexico.

Figure A-10
Petroglyph,
La Cieneguilla,
New Mexico.

Figure A-11
Petroglyph,
La Cieneguilla,
New Mexico.

Figure A-12
Petroglyph,
La Cieneguilla,
New Mexico.

Figure A-13
Petroglyph,
La Cieneguilla,
New Mexico.

Figure A-14
Petroglyph,
La Cieneguilla,
New Mexico.

Figure A-15
Petroglyphs,
La Cieneguilla,
New Mexico.

Figure A-16
Petroglyphs,
La Cieneguilla,
New Mexico.

Figure A-17 (left)
Petroglyph,
La Cieneguilla,
New Mexico.

Figure A-18 (left)
Petroglyph,
La Cieneguilla,
New Mexico.

*Figure A-19
Petroglyphs,
La Cieneguilla,
New Mexico.*

*Figure A-20
Petroglyph,
La Cieneguilla,
New Mexico.*

*Figure A-21
Petroglyphs,
La Cieneguilla,
New Mexico.*

*Figure A-22
Petroglyphs,
La Cieneguilla,
New Mexico.*

*Figure A-23
Petroglyphs,
La Cieneguilla,
New Mexico.*

*Figure A-24
Petroglyph,
La Cieneguilla,
New Mexico.*

*Figure A-25
Petroglyphs,
La Cieneguilla,
New Mexico.*

*Figure A-26
Petroglyphs,
La Cieneguilla,
New Mexico.*

*Figure A-27
Petroglyphs,
La Cieneguilla,
New Mexico.*

*Figure A-28 (left)
Petroglyph,
La Cieneguilla,
New Mexico.*

*Figure A-29 (left)
Petroglyphs,
La Cieneguilla,
New Mexico.*

Figure A-30
Petroglyph,
La Cieneguilla,
New Mexico.

Figure A-31
Petroglyph,
La Bajada Mesa,
New Mexico.

Figure A-32
Petroglyph,
Galisteo Basin,
New Mexico.

Figure A-33
Petroglyph,
Galisteo Basin,
New Mexico.

Figure A-34 (left)
Petroglyphs,
Galisteo Basin,
New Mexico.

Figure A-35 (right)
Petroglyphs,
Galisteo Basin,
New Mexico.

Figure A-36 (left)
Petroglyph panel,
Galisteo Basin,
New Mexico.

Figure A-37
Petroglyph,
Galisteo Basin,
New Mexico.

Figure A-38
Petroglyph panel,
Galisteo Basin,
New Mexico.

Figure A-39 (left)
Petroglyph,
Galisteo Basin,
New Mexico.

Figure A-40 (left)
Petroglyph panel,
Galisteo Basin,
New Mexico.

Figure A-41
Petroglyph,
Galisteo Basin,
New Mexico.

Figure A-42
Petroglyph panel,
Galisteo Basin,
New Mexico.

Figure A-43
Petroglyph panel,
Galisteo Basin,
New Mexico.

Figure A-45 (right)
Petroglyph,
Galisteo Basin,
New Mexico.
After photo by
Jeff Nelson.

Figure A-44
Petroglyph panel,
Galisteo Basin,
New Mexico.

Figure A-48 (left)
Petroglyph panel,
Galisteo Basin,
New Mexico.

Figure A-46
Petroglyph,
Galisteo Basin,
New Mexico.

Figure A-47
Petroglyph,
Galisteo Basin,
New Mexico.

Figure A-49 (left)
Petroglyph,
Galisteo Basin,
New Mexico.

Figure A-50 (left)
Petroglyph,
West Mesa,
Albuquerque,
New Mexico.
After Wellmann,
1979.

Figure A-51
Petroglyphs,
West Mesa,
Albuquerque.

Figure A-52
Petroglyphs,
West Mesa,
Albuquerque.

Figure A-53
Petroglyphs, West Mesa,
Albuquerque, New Mexico.

Figure A-54
Petroglyphs,
Tomé Hill,
New Mexico.

Figure A-55
Petroglyphs,
Tomé Hill,
New Mexico.

Figure A-56
Petroglyphs,
Tomé Hill,
New Mexico.

Figure A-57
Petroglyphs,
Tomé Hill,
New Mexico.

Figure A-58
(left)
Petroglyphs,
near Tenabó,
New Mexico.

Figure A-59
(left)
Petroglyphs,
near Tenabó,
New Mexico.

Figure A-60 (right)
Petroglyph,
Hidden Mountain,
New Mexico.

Figure A-61 (right)
Petroglyph,
near Chamita,
New Mexico.

Figure A-62 (left) and Figure A-63 (right)
Petroglyphs, north of Española, New Mexico.

Figure A-64
Petroglyphs, north of
Española, New Mexico.
After Boyd and
Ferguson, 1988.

Figure A-65
Petroglyphs, north of
Española,
New Mexico.

Figure A-68 (fright)
Petroglyphs, north of
Española,
New Mexico.

Figure A-67
Petroglyphs, north of
Española, New Mexico.

Figure A-66
Petroglyphs, north of
Española, New Mexico.

Figure A-69 (left)
Petroglyphs, north
of Española,
New Mexico.

Figure A-70
Petroglyphs, north
of Española,
New Mexico.
After Boyd and
Ferguson, 1988.

Figure A-72
(right)
Petroglyphs, north
of Española,
New Mexico.

Figure A-71
Petroglyphs, north of Española,
New Mexico.

Figure A-73 (left)
Petroglyphs, Holiday Mesa,
New Mexico.

*Figure A-74
Petroglyph,
San Juan Mesa,
New Mexico.
After Trask, 1992.*

*Figure A-75
Petroglyphs,
San Juan Mesa,
New Mexico.
After Trask, 1992.*

*Figure A-76
Petroglyph,
San Juan Mesa,
New Mexico.
After Trask, 1992.*

*Figure A-77
Petroglyph,
Tsankawi Ruin,
New Mexico.*

*Figure A-78
Petroglyph,
Tovakwa Ruin,
New Mexico.*

*Figure A-79
Petroglyphs, near Los Alamos, New Mexico.*

*Figure A-80
Petroglyphs, near Los Alamos,
New Mexico.*

*Figure A-83 (below)
Petroglyph,
White Rock Canyon,
New Mexico.*

*Figure A-82
Petroglyph,
White Rock
Canyon,*

*Figure A-81
Petroglyphs, near Los Alamos, New Mexico.*

*Figure A-84
(left)
Petroglyphs,
White Rock
Canyon,
New Mexico.*

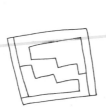

Figure A-85
Petroglyph, White Rock
Canyon, New Mexico.

Figure A-86
Petroglyph panel, north of
White Rock Canyon, New Mexico.

Figure A-87
Petroglyph panel, north of
White Rock Canyon, New Mexico.

Figure A-88
Petroglyph,
Abiquiu Reservoir,
New Mexico.
After Hibben, 1937.

Figure A-89
Pictograph panel,
Navajo Lake, New Mexico.
After Schaafsma, 1963.

Figure A-90
Petroglyph, near
Farmington,
New Mexico.
After Smith, 1974.

Figure A-91
Petroglyph panel,
near Farmington,
New Mexico.

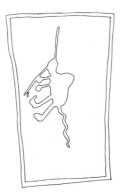

Figure A-94 (left)
Petroglyph,
Chaco Canyon area,
New Mexico.

Figure A-92
Petroglyph,
near Farmington,
New Mexico.
After Fallon, 1979.

Figure A-93
Petroglyph panel,
near Farmington,
New Mexico.

Figure A-95 (right)
Petroglyph panel, Chaco Canyon, New Mexico.
After file photo from National Park Service.

*Figure A-96
Petroglyphs,
Chaco Canyon, New Mexico.
After file photo from
National Park Service.*

*Figure A-97
Petroglyphs,
Chaco Canyon,
New Mexico.
After file photo from
National Park Service.*

*Figure A-98
Petroglyph,
Chaco Canyon,
New Mexico.
After file photo from
National Park
Service.*

*Figure A-99
Petroglyph,
Tapia Canyon,
New Mexico.*

*Figure A-100
(left)
Petroglyphs,
Tapia Canyon,
New Mexico.*

*Figure A-101
Petroglyphs, Tapia
Canyon,
New Mexico.*

*Figure A-102
Petroglyph,
Zuni Reservation,*

*Figure A-103
Petroglyph,
Zuni Reservation,
New Mexico.*

*Figure A-104
Petroglyph,
near Quemado,
New Mexico.*

*Figure A-105
Petroglyph,
Hardscrabble Wash,
Arizona.
After Young, 1988.*

*Figure A-106
Petroglyphs, Canyon de Chelly, Arizona.*

*Figure A-107 (left)
Petroglyph, Canyon de Chelly,
Arizona.
After Grant, 1978.*

Figure A-108
Petroglyph,
Canyon de Chelly,
Arizona.
After Grant, 1978.

Figure A-109
Pictograph,
Many Cherry
Canyon, Arizona.
After Grant, 1978.

Figure A-110
Pictograph,
Canyon de Chelly National
Monument, Arizona.
After Grant, 1978.

Figure A-111
Pictograph,
Canyon de Chelly
National Monument,
Arizona.
After Grant, 1978.

 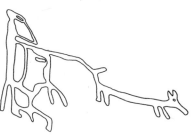 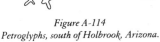

Figure A-112
Petroglyph, east
of Petrified Forest
National Park,
Arizona.
After Christensen,
1992.

Figure A-113
Petroglyphs, south of Holbrook, Arizona.

Figure A-114
Petroglyphs, south of Holbrook, Arizona.

Figure A-115
(left)
Petroglyphs,
south of
Holbrook,
Arizona.

Figure A-116
Petroglyphs, near Holbrook, Arizona.

Figure A-117
(left)
Petroglyphs,
near
Holbrook,
Arizona.

Figure A-118
Petroglyph panel, Walnut Canyon
National Monument, Arizona.
After Bruggmann, 1989.

*Figure A-120
(left)
Petroglyph
panel,
Wupatki
National
Monument,
Arizona.*

*Figure A-119
Petroglyphs, near
Wupatki National Monument,
Arizona. After Schaafsma, 1987.*

*Figure A-121
Pictograph,
Snake Gulch, Arizona.*

*Figure A-122
Petroglyph, west
of Kanab, Utah.*

*Figure A-123
Petroglyph, near
Overton, Nevada.
After L. Bringhurst,
Southern Nevada
Rock Art Enthusiasts
Newsletter, Autumn
1993.*

*Figure A-124
Petroglyph, near
confluence of
San Juan River and
Butler Wash, Utah.*

*Figure A-125 (left)
Petroglyphs, east of
Butler Wash, Utah.
After Castleton, 1987.*

*Figure A-126
Petroglyph, Butler Wash, Utah.*

*Figure A-128 (below)
Petroglyphs, Sand Island,
Utah. After Castleton, 1987.*

*Figure A-127
Petroglyphs,
Sand Island, Utah.
After Castleton, 1987.*

Figure A-129
Petroglyphs,
Sand Island, Utah.

Figure A-130 (left)
Petroglyphs, near
Bluff, Utah.

Figure A-131
Petroglyphs,
near Bluff, Utah.

Figure A-132
Petroglyphs,
southeastern Utah.
After Manning, 1990.

Figure A-133
Petroglyphs, near San Juan River, southeastern
Utah. After photo by Polly Schaafsma.

Figure A-134
Petroglyph, near
Bluff, Utah.
After photo by
Hugh Crouse.

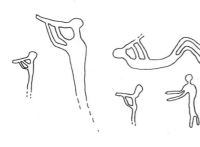

Figure A-135 (left)
Petroglyph panel,
near San Juan River
and Bluff, Utah.

Figure A-137
(above)
Pictograph,
Grand Gulch, Utah.
After Vuncannon, 1976.

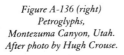

Figure A-136 (right)
Petroglyphs,
Montezuma Canyon, Utah.
After photo by Hugh Crouse.

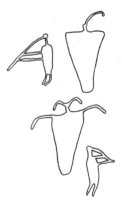

Figure A-139
Petroglyphs, Smith Fork, Utah (now submerged). After Foster, 1954.

Figure A-138
Petroglyph,
Johns Canyon, Utah.
After Castleton, 1987.

Figure A-141
Petroglyphs,
Glen Canyon
(lower Cha Canyon),
Utah.
After Turner, 1963.

Figure A-140
Petroglyphs, Glen Canyon
(Ticaboo Creek), Utah.
After Foster, 1954.

Figure A-142 (right)
Petroglyph, east of
Hall's Crossing, Utah.
After photo by
Margie Crouse.

Figure A-144
Petroglyph,
Indian Creek,
Utah.
After photo by
Hugh Crouse.

Figure A-145
Petroglyph,
Indian Creek,
Utah.
After photo by
Hugh Crouse.

Figure A-146
Petroglyph,
Indian Creek, Utah.

Figure A-143
Petroglyph panel, Indian
Creek drainage, Utah.
After Cole, 1990.

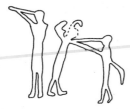

Figure A-147
Petroglyphs: fluteplayer with
"fighting" figures, near Moab,
Utah.

Figure A-148
Petroglyphs,
Canyonlands National Park,
Utah. After Castleton, 1987.

Figure A-149
Petroglyphs, Mussentuchit area, Utah.
After sketch by Jesse Warner.

Figure A-150
Petroglyph, Salt Wash,
Utah. After sketch
by Jesse Warner.

Figure A-151
Petroglyph, Molen Reef, Utah.

Figure A-152
Pictograph, Mesa
Verde area,
Colorado. After
Hayes, 1964.

Figure A-153
Petroglyph,
Mancos Canyon,
Colorado. After
Cole, 1990.

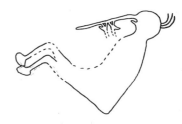

Figure A-155
Petroglyph, near Vernal,
Utah.

Figure A-154
Pictograph, Cañon Pintado,
Colorado.

Figure A-156
Petroglyph, near Vernal, Utah.
After photo by Hugh Crouse.

Figure A-157 (left)
and Figure A-158 (right)
Petroglyphs, near Vernal, Utah.
After photos by
Hugh Crouse.

Figure A-159
Petroglyph,
Dinosaur National
Monument, Utah.

Figure A-160
Petroglyph,
Dinosaur National
Monument, Utah.

*Figure A-161
Petroglyphs,
Dinosaur
National
Monument,
Utah.*

*Figure A-162
(left)
Petroglyph,
Three Rivers,
New Mexico.*

IMAGES IN CERAMICS AND KIVA MURALS

*Figure A-163
Humpbacked fluteplayer
from Mesa Verde bowl,
Colorado.
After Bruggmann, 1989.*

*Figure A-164
Kokopelli from Mesa
Verde bowl,
Colorado.
After Judd, 1954.*

*Figure A-165
Santa Fe Black-on-white sherd,
Paa-ko Ruin, New Mexico.
After Lambert, 1954.*

Index

(Note: page numbers in italic refer to illustration captions.)

Abajo-La Sal Style, 99, 161
Abiquiu Reservoir (NM), 59, *177*
Abo (NM), *174*
Abstract Style, 103, 161
Acoma, 4, 27, 123, 129
Algonkian Indians, 135
Alpert, Joyce, 28
American Rock Art Research Association, v
Anasazi, 3, 7, 19, *32*, 33, 37, 38, 74, 77, 83, 84, 91, 94, 100, 101, 103, 109, *111*
    area, 38-100
    Basketmaker Period, 4, 37, 39, 69, 71, 74, 75, 84, 91, 99-100, 162
    Kayenta, 83
    Pueblo Period, 4, 30, 37, 43, 49, 51, 52, 61, 71, 72, 73, 78, 79, 87, 91, 93, 109, 161, 165
    tradition, 3-4
    Western, 83
"Ancient Ones," 3, 33, 38
Andes (South America), 7
Antelope Mesa (AZ), *117*
anthropomorphs, 45, *46*, 60, *60*, *65*, 72, *73, 75, 76,* 77, 79, *80*, 81, *81, 83,* 84, *84, 85,* 86, *86,* 90, *90,* 91, *91, 92,* 93, 94, 95, *95, 96,* 97, *98,* 99, *99,* 101, 103, *104,* 106, 162

antiquity laws, 12
Apaches, 27, 32, 105
archaeological salvage, 94
Archaic Period, 74, 97, 101, 103, 106, 162, 168
Arrow Swallowers, 42, *43*, 45, *46*, 55, *56*. See also Stick Swallowers
arthritic men, in rock art, 91, *91*
Asa Clan, 24
Ashley Creek (UT), 101
Assiniboine Indians, 135
Awanyu, 162
Awatovi (Hopi), 104, 110, 115, 116, *117*
Aztec Canyon (AZ), *106*
Aztecs, 4, 25

backpacker figures, *93, 96*, 102
Bandelier National Monument, 56, 58, *58*
Barrier Canyon Anthropomorphic Style, 97, *97*, 98, *98*, 101, 162
basket, burden, 26
Basketmaker Period. See Anasazi
Beaver Flattop Mountains, 100
Behind the Rocks area (UT), 95
Betatakin, 8
bighorn sheep, 86, *86*, 87, 98, *98, 111*
bird bone, 19
bird symbolism, 74
birth scene, 62, *63*, 68, *68, 89*
Bluff (UT), 32, 89, *89, 90*, 91, *181*
Brown's Park (CO), 101
bullet holes, on rock art, 11
Butler Wash (UT), *32,* 84, *85*, 86, *86*, 87, *180*

Cable Cave (AZ), 73
carbon-14 (C-14) dating, 97-98, 162
canes, in rock art, 7, 32, *32, 33, 87*, 90
Cañon Pintado National Historic District, 100, *183*
Canyon de Chelly (AZ), 4, *23*, 24, *24*, 70, 71-73, *71-73, 178, 179*
Canyon del Muerto (AZ), *38*, 73
Canyonlands National Park, 97, 98, *183*
Capitol Reef National Park, 75, 102, *102*
Casas Grandes (Chihuahua, Mexico), 4, 7
Cave Kiva (NM), 53, *56*
Cave Valley Style, 83, *83,* 84, 162
Cave Valley (UT), *84*
Cedar Mesa (UT), 91
Cedar Mountain (UT), 98, *98*
ceramics, and fluteplayer images, 109-115

Cerro Indio (NM), 52
Cha Canyon (UT), 93, *182*
Chaco Canyon, 4, 26, 62, 63, *63*, 64, *64*, 65, 115, *115*, 116, *116*, *177*, *178*
Chaco Culture National Historic Park, 62
chalk, misuse of, 11
Chamita (NM), 52, *174*
Chapin Mesa (Mesa Verde National Park), 99
Chihuahua, Mexico, 4, 103
Chihuahuan Desert, 7
Chinle Wash (UT), 90, *91*
Chu'lu'laneh, 68
Chumash Indian sites, 12
Chuska Mountains, 61, *62*
Classic Vernal Style, 101, 163, 168
clay figurines, 97
"Clay's Tablet," 142
Cloud Blower, 42, *42*
cloud terraces, 117
Clown Society, 132
Cochiti Pueblo (NM), 59, *59*
Cocopeli, ix-x
Cocopeli Stories, x
Colorado Plateau, 7, 38
Colorado River, 4, 10, 84, 92, 100
Comanche Cave (TX), 105
Comb Ridge (UT), 86, *87*
"Coming of the Gods" ceremony, 40
Cooke's Peak (NM), 103, *104*
copulation scene, *81*
corn, pod, 8. See also maize, tunicate
Coronado, expedition of, 20
Cuba (NM), 65
Cub Creek (Dinosaur National Monument), 101
culture groups, southwestern prehistoric, chronology of, *6*

Dinosaur National Monument, 101, *184*
Dolores River, 10, 110, *111*
Douglas Creek (CO), 100
Dry Fork (UT), 101
Durango (CO), 99, *100*

Eagle Man, 27
Ek Chuah, 25
El Paso (TX), 105
emetics, 42
Española (NM), north of, *20, 23,* 26,52, *52, 53, 54, 55, 169, 175*
Esteban, 131

Farmington (NM), 60, *61, 177*
fertility context, 110, 117
Fewkes, Jesse Walter, 24
Fire Temple (Mesa Verde National Park), 22, 117
Fivemile Draw (AZ), 26
Flagstaff (AZ), 79
Flute Clan, 24-25
flute, of Kokopelli, 19-20, 87
fluteplayer-animal relationship, 24
Fluteplayer Cave, 72, 79
Fluteplayer Rock, 63, *64*
Fluteplayer Shrine, 56, *57*
flute societies (Hopi), 21
Fort Hancock (TX), 105, *105*
Four Corners region, 5, 10, 28, 32, 95, 101
Fox Indians, 135
Fredonia (AZ), 83
Fremont culture, 4, 37, 38, 100-102, *103*, 163

Galisteo Basin, 26, 40, 43, 45, *45, 46, 47, 48, 172, 173*
Gallup Black-on-white, 112, *113*
Gallup (NM), 65, *66, 67*
Ghanaskidi, 27, 31, *31*, 32, 61, 135
Gila Butte phase, 113-114
Glen Canyon, 25, *93, 94, 182*
Glooscap, 135
Gobernador Phase, 32, 163
"Golden Age" of southwestern rock art, 2
graffiti, on rock art, 11
Grand Gulch (UT), 91, *91, 92, 181*
Grant, Campbell, 24
gray desert-robber fly, and Kokopelli, 21
Great Salt Lake culture area, 100, 163
Green River, 10, 97
Green River (UT), 98
Gros Ventre Indians, 135

Hall's Crossing (UT), *182*
Hano, 26, 131
Hardscrabble Wash (AZ), 69, *69, 70, 178*
Hare, 135
Haury, Emil W., 105
Hidden Mountain (NM), 52, *174*
Hidden Valley (CO), 99
Hohokam culture, 4, 7, 31, 32, 37, 83, 105-106, 163
    ceramic motifs, 26, *26*, 30, *30*, 106, 113-114, 139

Hohokam culture (continued)
    Classic Period, 105
Holbrook (AZ), 69, 74, 75, *75, 76, 170, 179*
Holiday Mesa (NM), 55, *56, 130, 175*
Homol'ovi State Park, 77, *77*
Hopi, 4, 8, 10, 21, 24, 26, 27, 31, 40, 42, 55, 83, 104, 123-126
Hopi Flute Kachina, 28
Hopi Flute Society, 21
Horseshoe Canyon (Canyonlands National Park), 97
horticulture, in the Southwest, 103
Hueco Tanks (TX), *33*, 105
humpbacked fluteplayer, 2-10, 24, 26-29, 45, 46. See also Kokopelli
hunter-warrior aspect, 22
hunting-magic context, 78, *78*, 94, *98*, 116, *116*, 117
hunting-priest aspect, 22

iconography, 163
Iktomi, 135
Indian Creek drainage (UT), 94, *94*, 95, *182*
insectiform, 163
insects, and Kokopelli, 21, 30, 45, 52, *54*, 69, *69*, 134. See also insectiform
International Rock Art Congress, v
irrigation systems, 105
Ishtinike, 135
Island in the Sky District (Canyonlands National Park), 97
Isleta Pueblo, 49, *50*

Jalisco, Mexico, 106
Jemez Mountains, 53, 56, 59, 129
Jemez Pueblo, 117, *118*
Jemez Springs (NM), 55, 56
Johns Canyon (UT), 91, *92, 182*
Johnson, Clay, 142
Jornada phase, 32, 51, 103, 124
Jornada Style, 103, 104, 164
Jung, Carl, 136

kachina, 8, 10, 24, 28, 31, 40, 74, 77, 123-126
kachina cult, 8, 123-124
Kanab (UT), 84, *84, 180*
Kayenta (AZ), 78, 79, *80*
Keet Seel Ruin (AZ), 78
kiva murals, and fluteplayer images, 109, 115-119
Kokopelli, vi, 2, 3, 15-16, 17, 35-36, 39, 40, 57, 59, 78, 91, 92, 104, 105, 110, 121, 141
    and bird images, 26

and his flute, 19-20
and his hump, 26-29
and Pott's disease, 28-29
as an insect, 134
as a Zuni kachina, 130-132
as Trickster, 134-136
attributes of, 18
character depictions of, 18
complexity of his character, 33
cult, 61
fertility role of, 22, *24*
kachina, 24, 123-126
kachina dance, 125-126
kachina doll, *125*
migrations of, 24-26
myths of, 123-136
name variations of, 8
origin of, 7, 8, 24-26
relatives of, 30-33
roles of, 3, 20-24
stories of, 123-136
traits of, 3
variations in style and concept, 38
variety of images of, 17-18
zoomorphic attributes of. See zoomorphic attributes of fluteplayers
"Kokopelli Kitsch," 137
"Kokopelli's Return," 121
Kokopelli Trail, 139
Kokopelmana, 111, 112, 116-117, 126-127, 136
kyphosis, 29

La Bajada Mesa (NM), *43, 172*
La Cienega, 42, *42, 43*, 132, 133, *133, 169*
La Cieneguilla (NM), *19, 20, 21*, 22, 26, *27*, 28, *28, 33*, 39, *39, 40*, 41, *41, 170, 171, 172*
Lake Powell, 92
Largo Canyon (NM), *31*, 32, 61, *61, 62*
La Sal Creek Canyon (CO), 99, *99*
Last Chance Canyon (UT), *93*
Ledge Ruin, 73
Lenang, 28
Little Colorado River, 10, 75, 103
locusts, and Kokopelli, 21, 134
Long House Valley (AZ), 78
Los Alamos (NM), 53
Los Alamos Canyon, 56, 57, *176*

Los Lunas, 49, 52
Los Padres National Forest (CA), 12

macaws, 56. See also parrots
Main Canyon (UT), 102
maize, tunicate, 8
Mancos Black-on-white, 110, *111*
Mancos Canyon (CO), 99, *183*
Many Cherry Canyon (AZ), 72, *179*
Marcos de Niza, 131
Marsh Pass (AZ), *19, 29, 78*
Meeker (CO), 100
Mesa Verde National Park, 99, 110, *110*, 117, *183, 184*
Mesoamerica, 25-26, 28, 105-106
Mexico, 4, 7
Mill Creek (UT), 95
Mimbres culture, 4, 32, 33, 103, 114-115, 164, *169*
Moab (UT), 72, *72*, 95, *96*, 97, *183*
Moctezuma, 28
Mogollon culture, 4, 7, 8, 20, 30, 32, 33, 37, 83, 103-105, 124, 164
Mogollon Red Style, 103, 164
Molen Reef (UT), 98, *183*
Montezuma Canyon (UT), 91, *181*
Monticello (UT), 94
Monument Valley (AZ), 77-78, *78*
Mountainair (NM), 51
Mountain Piro district, 51
Mussentuchit area (UT), 98, *98, 183*

Nanabozho, 135
National Park Service, 13
Natural Bridges National Monument, 91
Navajo, 30, 31, 59, 61, 71
Navajo Lake, 59, *60, 177*
Navajo National Monument (AZ), *19*, 78
Navajo Night Chant myth, 32
Neary, John, 137
Nepayatamu, 131, 132
Nepokwa'i, 131
Nevada, 38
Nine Mile Canyon (UT), 102, *102*
Nixant, 135
Northern San Rafael Style, 164
Northwest Coast Indians, 135

Oglala-Sioux Indians, 135

Ololowishkya, 130, *130*
Oraibi, 25
Orpheus, 136
Otowi Bridge (NM), 58
Ouray (UT), 102
Overton (NV), 84, *180*
Owiwi, 130

Paa-ko (NM), 113, *184*
Page (AZ), 78
Paiyatamu, 68, 130, 131
Paleo-Indian Period, 164
Pan, 136
Pang, 31, 32
Papago Indians. See Tohono O'Odham
Parowan culture area, 100, 165
parrots, 61
Patterson-Rudolph, 42
Pecos River, 38, 103
Petrified Forest National Park (AZ), 72, *72*, 73, *73, 74, 179*
Petroglyph National Monument (NM), 48
petroglyphs, 2, 165
phallic figures, *32, 33*, 41, 44, *44*, 45, *46*, 48, *49*, 52, *54*, 55, 57, 60, 61, *63*,
 68, *70*, 72, 73, 75, *75*, 78, 84, *86*, 87, *87, 88*, 89, *89*, 90, *94, 96*, 97, 99,
 104, 105, *105*, 110, *112*, 115, 116, 117, 118, 133, *135*
Phoenix (AZ), 106, *106*
pictographs, 2, 165
Pima Indians, 106
pit houses, 103
Polychrome Style, 165
pochtecas, 4, 7, 26
Ponca Indians, 135
Pott's disease, 28-29
priapism, 29, 35
Price (UT), 102
Procession Panel, 86, *87*
Pueblo I black-on-white, 110, *110*
Pueblo Indians, 7, 20, 86
Pueblo Period. See Anasazi
Pueblo Revolt, 116
Puerco Ruin, 73

Quemado (NM), *27*, 68, *68, 178*
Quetzalcoatl, 28

rain symbolism, *92*

Raven, 135
reeds, for flutes, 20
Representational Style, 165
Reserve (NM), 103
Reserve Petroglyph Style, 103, 165
Rio Grande River, 4, 10, 24, 52, 57, 58, *58*, 104
    pueblos of, 7, 51
Rio Grande Style, 39, 69, 124, 166
Rio Grande Valley, 38, 59, 124
Rio Puerco (NM), 65, 73
rock art
    fluteplayer images in, 37-106
    how to protect, 11-13
    Navajo, 32
    origins of, 1
    purposes of, 1
    sites
        general locations of, 10
        map of, *9*
        visiting of, 10-13
    stylistic elements in, 2
rubbings, misuse of, 11
Russell, Sharman Apt, 16

Sacaton Red-on-buff, *114*
Salt River (AZ), 106
Salt Wash (UT), 98, *183*
Sand Canyon (CO), 118, *119*
Sandia Mountains (NM), 113
Sand Island, 32, *32*, 87, *88*, 89, *89, 180, 181*
San Juan Anthropomorphic Style, 84, 166
San Juan Basin, 26
San Juan Basketmaker Style, 86
San Juan Mesa (NM), 56, *176*
San Juan River, 4, 10, 59, 84, 85-86, *86*, 87, 90, 91, 92, *180, 181*
San Rafael culture area, 100
San Rafael River, 98
San Rafael Style, 166
Santa Fe, 22, 37, 43, 52, 53, 139
Santa Fe Black-on-white, 112-113, *184*
Santa Fe River Canyon, 22
Schaafsma, Polly, 30, 39
Second Mesa (Hopi), 124
Sevenmile Canyon (UT), *96*, 97, *97*
Sevier cultural region, 100, 166
Shalako kachinas, **40**, 166

shamanistic activities, 23, 74, 95
Shay Canyon (UT), *95*
She Who Remembers, 107
Shiprock (NM), 61
Shuler, Linda Lay, 107
Sierra Estrella (AZ), 106, *106*
Silver, Constance S., 115
Sinagua culture, 4, 83, 167
Sitconski, 135
Sityatki Polychrome, 110, *112*, 166-167
Sleeping Duck Ruin (AZ), 72
Smith Fork (UT), 93, *182*
smoke damage, on rock art, 12
Snake Gulch (AZ), 83, *83*, 84, *180*
snake swallowing, 42
Snaketown (AZ), 30, *30*, 105, 113
social dynamics, and rock art, vii
Songs of the Fluteplayer, 15-16
Sonora, Mexico, 103
soul-flight, 74, 95
South America, 4, 7
Southern San Rafael Style, 167
South Mountain (AZ), 106, *106*
Southwest (U.S.), 7, *9*, 19, 25, 74, 93-94, 103, 123, 136
Spanish, 3, 37
Spider Clan, 25
St. George (UT), 84
Stick Swallowers, 42, 45

Tapia Canyon (NM), *66, 178*
Tenabó Ruin (NM), 51, *51, 174*
Tewa, 167
Third Mesa (Hopi), 124
Three Rivers (NM), 104, 105, *105*, 116-117, *117, 184*
Ticaboo Creek (UT), 93, *182*
Titmouse Clan, 25
Tohono O'Odham Indians, 106
Tomé Hill (NM), 49, *174*
Tompiro district, 51, 52, 167
Tonque Arroyo, 49, *50*
Tovakwa Ruin (NM), 56, *176*
Towler, Solala, x
trade networks, 7, 25-26
Trail Canyon (UT), 93, *94*
Trickster, the, 134-136
trocador, 26

Tsankawi Ruin (NM), 56, *176*
Tsegi Canyon (AZ), 8, 79, *79*
Tunnel Canyon (AZ), 71
twinned fluteplayers, *65, 71. 73, 84*
Tziguma, 39

Uinta culture region, 100, 101, 167-168
Uncompahgre River drainage (CO), *169*
U.S. Bureau of Land Management, 13
U.S. Forest Service, 13
Utah Rock Art Research Association, v
Ute Mountain Tribal Park, 99
Uto-Aztecan language, 106

Valley of Fire State Park, 84
Vernal (UT), 101, *183*
Village of the Great Kivas (NM), 112
Virgin Kayenta branch, 168

Wakdjunkaga, 135, 136
Walnut Canyon National Monument (NM), 79, 83, *179*
warrior societies, 42
War Twins, 86
Water Clan, 25
Water Jar Boy myth, 42, 132-134
Webb, G. B., 28
Wellmann, Klaus F., 28
West Mesa (Albuquerque, NM), 26, 48, *49, 50, 173, 174*
White River, 100
White Rock Canyon (NM), 57, *58, 176, 177*
Williams, Terry Tempest, 121
Willow Creek (UT), 102
Wind in the Rock, 36
Winnebago tribe, 135
Winslow (AZ), 77
Wisaka, 135
Wupatki National Monument, 79, 81, *81, 82*, 83, *180*

Xochiquetzal, 28

ye'i, 31, 32
Yellow Jacket Canyon (CO), 118

zoomorphic attributes of fluteplayers, *23, 32*, 44, *60*, 61, *64, 65*, 79, *82*, 87, 168

Zuni (NM), 2, 4, 21, 24, 27, 40, 67, *67*, 68, *68*, 69, 112, *112*, 123, 124, *130*, *178*
    kachina, 130-132
Zwinger, Ann, 36

LOCATIONS OF ROCK ART SITES LISTED IN BOOK

Abiquiu Reservoir (NM), 59, 177
Abo (NM), 174
Ashley Creek (UT), 101
Aztec Canyon (AZ), 106
Bandelier National Monument (NM), 56, 58
Beaver Flattop Mountains (CO), 100
Behind the Rocks (UT), 95
Bluff (UT), 32, 89, 90, 91, 181
Brown's Park (CO), 101
Butler Wash (UT), 32, 84, 85, 86, 87, 180
Cable Cave (AZ), 73
Cañon Pintado National Historic District (CO), 100, 183
Canyon de Chelly National Monument, 4, 23, 24, 70, 71-73, 178, 179
Canyon del Muerto (AZ), 38, 70
Canyonlands National Park (UT), 97, 98, 183
Capitol Reef National Park (UT), 75, 102
Cave Kiva (NM), 53, 56
Cave Valley (UT), 84
Cedar Mesa (UT), 91
Cedar Mountain (UT), 98
Cerro Indio (NM), 52
Cha Canyon (UT), 93, 182
Chaco Canyon (NM), 4, 26, 62, 63, 64, 65, 115, 116, 177, 178
Chamita (NM), 52, 174
Chapin Mesa (Mesa Verde National Park), 99
Chinle Wash (UT), 90, 91
Chuska Mountains (NM), 61, 62
Cochiti Pueblo (NM), 59
Comanche Cave (TX), 105
Comb Ridge (UT), 86, 87
Cooke's Peak (NM), 103, 104
Cuba (NM), 65
Cub Creek (Dinosaur National Monument), 101
Dinosaur National Monument, 101, 184
Douglas Creek (CO), 100
Dry Fork (UT), 101
Durango (CO), 99, 100
Española (NM), north of, 20, 23, 52, 53, 54, 55, 169, 175

Farmington (NM), 60, 61, 177
Fivemile Draw (AZ), 26, Color Plate 1
Fluteplayer Cave (AZ), 72, 79
Fort Hancock (TX), 105
Galisteo Basin, 26, 40, 43, 45, 46, 47, 48, 172, 173
Gallup (NM), 65, 66, 67
Glen Canyon area, 25, 93, 94, 182
Grand Gulch (UT), 91, 92, 181
Hall's Crossing (UT), 182
Hardscrabble Wash (AZ), 69, 70, 178
Hidden Mountain (NM), 52, 174
Hidden Valley (CO), 99
Holbrook (AZ), 69, 74, 75, 76, 170, 179
Holiday Mesa (NM), 55, 56, 130, 175
Homol'ovi State Park (AZ), 77
Horseshoe Canyon (Canyonlands National Park), 97
Hueco Tanks (TX), 33, 105
Indian Creek drainage (UT), 94, 95, 182
Isleta Pueblo, 49, 50
Johns Canyon (UT), 91, 92
Kanab (UT), 84, 180
Kayenta (AZ), 78, 79, 80
Keet Seel Ruin (AZ), 78
La Bajada Mesa (NM), 43, 172
La Cienega (NM), 42, 43, 132, 133, 169
La Cieneguilla (NM), 19, 20, 21, 22, 27, 28, 33, 39, 40, 41, 170, 171, 172
Largo Canyon (NM), 31, 32, 61, 62
La Sal Creek Canyon (CO), 99
Last Chance Canyon (UT), 93
Ledge Ruin (AZ), 73
Long House Valley (AZ), 78
Los Alamos Canyon, 56, 57, 176
Main Canyon (UT), 102
Mancos Canyon (CO), 99, 183
Many Cherry Canyon (AZ), 72, 179
Marsh Pass (AZ), 19, 29, 78
Mesa Verde National Park (CO), 99, 110, 183, 184
Mill Creek (UT), 95
Moab (UT), 72, 95, 96, 97, 183
Molen Reef (UT), 98, 183
Montezuma Canyon (UT), 91, 181
Monument Valley (AZ), 77, 78
Mussentuchit area (AZ/UT), 98, 183
Natural Bridges National Monument, 91
Navajo Lake, 59, 60, 177
Navajo National Monument (AZ), 19, 78

Nine Mile Canyon (UT), 102
Overton (NV), 84, 180
Petrified Forest National Park, 72, 73, 74, 179
Puerco Ruin (AZ), 73
Quemado (NM), 27, 68, 178
Reserve (NM), 103
Rio Puerco (NM), 65, 73
Salt Wash (UT), 98, 183
Sand Island (UT), 32, 87, 88, 89, 180, 181
San Juan Mesa (NM), 56, 176
San Juan River (UT), 4, 10, 59, 84, 85, 86, 87, 90, 91, 92, 180, 181
Santa Fe River Canyon (NM), 22
Sevenmile Canyon (UT), 96, 97
Shay Canyon (UT), 95
Shiprock (NM), 61
Sierra Estrella (AZ), 106
Sleeping Duck Ruin, 72
Smith Fork (UT), 93, 182
Snake Gulch (AZ), 83, 84, 180
South Mountain (AZ), 106
St. George (UT), 84
Tapia Canyon (NM), 66, 178
Tenabó Ruin (NM), 51, 174
Three Rivers (NM), 104, 105, 116, 117, 184
Ticaboo Creek (UT), 93, 182
Tomé Hill (NM), 49, 174
Tonque Arroyo (NM), 49, 50
Tovakwa Ruin (NM), 56, 176
Trail Canyon (UT), 93, 94
Tsankawi Ruin (NM), 56, 176
Tsegi Canyon (AZ), 8, 79
Tunnel Canyon (AZ), 71
Uncompahgre River drainage, 169
Ute Mountain Tribal Park (CO), 99
Valley of Fire State Park (NV), 84
Vernal (UT), 101, 102, 183
Walnut Canyon National Monument, 79, 83, 179
West Mesa (NM), 49, 50, 173, 174
White Rock Canyon (NM), 57, 58, 176, 177
Winslow (AZ), 77
Wupatki National Monument, 79, 81, 82, 83, 180
Zuni Reservation (NM), 2, 4, 21, 24, 27, 40, 67, 68, 69, 112, 123, 124, 130, 178

THE AUTHORS

Dennis Slifer is a geologist with the New Mexico Environment Department in Santa Fe. An early interest in cave exploring in the Appalachians introduced him to the fascination of prehistoric archaeological sites. In addition to his professional interest in rocks, his avocational concern with rock art dates back to the 1970s.

Slifer first encountered the mystery of petroglyphs while conducting geologic field work in the desert as a graduate student at the University of Colorado. Rock art has been the focus of many of his outings throughout the Southwest since that time. His visiting and photographing hundreds of rock art sites, with a special attention to fluteplayer images, eventually led to production of this book. His previous publications include The Caves of Maryland and numerous environmental reports.

A serendipitous encounter with James Duffield several years ago at a remote pueblo ruin in the Galisteo Basin of New Mexico forged the liaison that resulted in the publication of this work.

James Duffield, also a geologist, by education if not by profession, has worked in the travel industry since 1960. This has enabled him to indulge his fascination with ancient history and archaeology by allowing him to visit many sites around the globe. He completed two years of graduate study in Classical Archaeology at New York University and spent two summers as a field archaeologist at a Late Roman site in western Turkey.

Since his move to Santa Fe in 1975, Duffield has developed a keen interest in southwestern archaeology. During the past several years this interest (inspired by coauthor Dennis Slifer) has become focused on rock art documentation and photography, with an emphasis on fluteplayer images.

Dennis Slifer

James Duffield